Motivational Interviewing for Beginners

A Step-by-Step Guide to Creating Meaningful Change

Jane W. Harlow

Copyright © 2024 by Jane W. Harlow. All rights reserved.

First Edition

ISBN: 978-1-7637425-4-3

Table of Contents

Preface 1
Chapter 1: Introduction to Motivational Interviewing (MI) 3
    What is Motivational Interviewing? 3
    History and Origin of MI 4
    Why MI is Useful 5
Chapter 2: Core Principles of MI 11
    Partnership 11
    Acceptance 13
    Compassion 15
    Evocation 16
Chapter 3: The Spirit of MI 20
    Empathy 20
    Active Listening 22
    Collaboration 23
    Understanding Ambivalence 25
Chapter 4: The Four Processes of MI 31
    Engaging 31
    Focusing 33
    Evoking 35
    Planning 37
Chapter 5: The OARS Model of MI 42
    Open-ended Questions 42

    Affirmations 44

    Reflective Listening 46

    Summarizing 48

Chapter 6: Change Talk and Sustain Talk in MI 60

    What is Change Talk? 60

    What is Sustain Talk? 62

Chapter 7: Developing a Change Plan 72

    Moving from Motivation to Action 72

    Creating a Collaborative Change Plan 76

Chapter 8: Real-Life Applications of MI 86

    MI in Health Settings 86

    MI in Coaching and Mentorship 89

    MI in Education and Social Work 93

    Case Studies and Examples 96

Chapter 9: Common Mistakes in MI 100

    The Righting Reflex 100

    Overloading the Conversation 102

    Not Allowing Enough Time for the Person to Reflect . 104

Chapter 10: Practicing MI in Everyday Life 114

    Integrating MI into Daily Conversations 115

    Building Confidence Through Practice 121

Conclusion 128

Reference 134

Preface

Welcome! If you're holding this book, it's likely because you've heard about Motivational Interviewing (MI) and want to understand how it can help create positive changes in people's lives—whether in your personal relationships, workplace, or community. You might be a counselor, a coach, a healthcare worker, a social worker, or someone who simply wants to help others make better decisions. No matter who you are, this book is for you.

Motivational Interviewing (MI) can feel like a complex technique when you first come across it, but my goal is to make it easy for you to learn and apply. This book is written with beginners in mind, using a simple and easy-to-follow approach. It's not packed with technical jargon or complicated theories. Instead, it's a step-by-step guide to understanding the key MI techniques and how to use them in real life.

You'll learn how to have effective, supportive conversations with people who are feeling stuck or unsure about making changes. MI isn't about telling someone what to do—it's about helping them explore their own motivations, understand their ambivalence, and find the courage to take the next step.

Each chapter is filled with real-life examples, practical tips, and exercises you can use to build your confidence in using MI. You'll discover how MI works in different settings, from healthcare and addiction recovery to coaching, social work, and even in day-to-day conversations with friends or family.

By the end of this book, you will have a solid grasp of how to use Motivational Interviewing in a way that feels natural, compassionate, and effective. More importantly, you'll be ready to help others move toward meaningful change in their own lives.

I hope you find this guide useful, practical, and inspiring as you embark on your journey to learn Motivational Interviewing. Let's get started!

Jane W. Harlow

Chapter 1: Introduction to Motivational Interviewing (MI)

What is Motivational Interviewing?

Motivational Interviewing (MI) is a communication technique designed to help people change their behavior by tapping into their intrinsic motivations. Simply put, MI is a way of having conversations that encourage individuals to talk about their own reasons for change rather than feeling like they are being told what to do. This approach is particularly helpful when someone feels ambivalent or unsure about making a change in their life.

Imagine you're trying to help a friend quit smoking. Instead of lecturing them about the dangers of smoking or insisting that they quit immediately, you might ask questions like, "What do you enjoy about smoking?" or "What would life look like for you if you stopped?" This way, your friend gets to explore their own feelings about smoking and think about what might motivate them to quit. That's what MI is all about—guiding people to uncover their personal reasons for making positive changes.

In Motivational Interviewing, the focus is on being empathetic, listening carefully, and avoiding judgment. The idea is not to force someone into making a change but to help them discover why making a change could be beneficial for them.

In MI, change is viewed as a process. People aren't always ready to make big changes overnight, and that's okay. MI helps them work through their thoughts and feelings until they feel ready to take action.

History and Origin of MI

Motivational Interviewing was first developed in the 1980s by two clinical psychologists, William R. Miller and Stephen Rollnick. It all started when William Miller noticed something interesting while working with clients who struggled with alcohol addiction. Miller observed that when he spoke with these individuals in a way that was non-judgmental, empathetic, and supportive, they were more likely to talk openly about their drinking habits and even begin thinking about making changes. Instead of being defensive or resistant, these clients seemed to become more open to change.

Miller began to realize that pushing or pressuring clients to change didn't work. Instead, the key was to help them explore their own reasons for wanting to change and support them through the process. Motivational Interviewing was born out of this insight and was later refined by Miller and Rollnick in their collaboration.

The first official description of Motivational Interviewing appeared in Miller's 1983 article published in the journal "Behavioral Psychotherapy." In the years that followed, MI gained attention and started being used in various fields beyond addiction treatment, including healthcare, counseling, and even education.

Miller and Rollnick continued to develop the approach, and in 1991, they published their first book, "Motivational Interviewing: Preparing People to Change Addictive

Behavior." This book was a milestone in the field and has since been updated and expanded to include broader applications of MI.

Today, MI is widely recognized as an effective tool for promoting behavior change across many different areas of life, and it has been adapted and used in settings ranging from medical clinics to counseling sessions to coaching environments.

Why MI is Useful
Real-Life Applications in Healthcare, Counseling, Coaching, etc.

Motivational Interviewing is useful because it helps people address their ambivalence about change. Ambivalence means feeling two different ways about something, like when someone knows that smoking is bad for them but also enjoys it and feels comforted by it. MI is particularly helpful for people who feel stuck in this kind of push-pull between wanting to change and not being sure if they can or should.

Here are some of the many areas where MI has proven to be especially useful:

---

1. Healthcare

In healthcare, MI is often used to help patients make lifestyle changes that will improve their health. This might include changes like quitting smoking, losing weight, managing diabetes, or reducing alcohol consumption. Healthcare professionals, such as doctors, nurses, and dietitians, can use MI to have conversations that help patients explore their motivations for making these changes.

For example, let's say a doctor is talking to a patient who is at risk for heart disease due to their diet and lack of exercise. Instead of simply telling the patient to eat better and exercise more, the doctor might say, "What do you enjoy about the foods you're eating now?" and "How do you feel about getting more active?" This encourages the patient to reflect on their own lifestyle and think about how changes might benefit them.

MI helps healthcare professionals avoid the trap of giving advice that might not stick. By focusing on the patient's own motivations and allowing them to express any concerns or hesitations, MI helps foster a sense of personal responsibility and empowerment.

2. Addiction Treatment and Counseling

MI was originally developed for helping people with addiction, and it remains one of the most effective tools for addiction treatment today. When someone struggles with addiction, they often feel torn between wanting to quit and wanting to continue using the substance they are addicted to. MI helps people resolve this ambivalence by guiding them to explore their reasons for quitting and how their life might improve if they did.

In a counseling session, a therapist might use MI by asking a client who is trying to stop drinking, "What's one thing you enjoy about not drinking?" and "How do you feel the next day after a night of drinking?" These types of questions get the client thinking about both the pros and cons of drinking, which can help them see more clearly why quitting might be a positive choice.

Real-life example: Jessica has been struggling with alcohol use for years. She enjoys socializing with friends over drinks, but she also hates how drinking makes her feel afterward, and she knows it's affecting her health. In a counseling session, her therapist uses MI to help her weigh her options. Instead of telling Jessica to quit drinking right away, the therapist asks, "How do you feel when you're able to go out without drinking? What would it be like to have more control over your drinking?" These questions help Jessica think about the benefits of cutting back and start to shift her mindset toward positive change.

3. Coaching and Mentorship

Motivational Interviewing is not just for healthcare and counseling; it's also an incredibly useful tool for coaches and mentors who want to help their clients achieve their goals. Whether it's in career coaching, life coaching, or sports coaching, MI can help individuals unlock their potential by focusing on their inner motivations.

Imagine a career coach working with a client who feels stuck in their job but is unsure about making a career change. Instead of pushing the client to make a decision right away, the coach might use MI to explore the client's feelings. They might ask, "What do you like about your current job?" and "What would your ideal job look like?" These questions help the client explore their values and motivations, making it easier for them to take action when they're ready.

Real-life example: David, a 35-year-old IT professional, feels unfulfilled in his current job, but he's not sure if he should leave. During a session with his career coach, the coach uses MI techniques to help David explore his feelings about his job. "What are some things you enjoy about your work?" the coach asks. David responds that he enjoys solving problems and working with technology but dislikes the long hours and lack of growth opportunities. The coach then asks, "If you could design your perfect job, what would it include?" This gets David thinking about the types of roles that align with his skills and interests, and he begins to consider options for making a career change.

---

4. Education and Social Work

In education and social work, MI can be used to help students and clients navigate challenges and make positive choices. Teachers, school counselors, and social workers often work with individuals who are facing difficult circumstances and may be struggling to find motivation for change.

For example, a social worker might use MI to help a teenager who is at risk of dropping out of school. Instead of lecturing the teen about the importance of staying in school, the social worker might ask, "What do you enjoy about school when it's going well?" and "How would finishing school help you achieve your future goals?" This approach encourages the teenager to reflect on the benefits of staying in school and may help them feel more motivated to succeed.

Real-life example: Sara, a 16-year-old student, is falling behind in her classes and is thinking about dropping out. Her school counselor, instead of giving her a lecture about why she should stay in school, uses MI to engage Sara in a conversation about her future. "What are some things you enjoy doing outside of school?" the counselor asks. Sara mentions her love for art and design, which leads to a discussion about how finishing school could open up opportunities for her to pursue a career in graphic design. By focusing on Sara's interests and goals, the counselor helps her see the value in continuing her education.

5. Managing Chronic Conditions

People living with chronic health conditions, such as diabetes or heart disease, often need to make lifestyle changes to manage their illness effectively. However, these changes can be challenging, especially when they involve long-term commitments like following a strict diet or exercise regimen. MI can be particularly helpful in these cases by helping individuals find their own reasons for sticking with these changes.

For example, a nurse might work with a patient who has diabetes and needs to change their eating habits. Instead of telling the patient what they should and shouldn't eat, the nurse might use MI to ask, "How do you feel when your blood sugar is well-controlled?" and "What are some small changes you think you could make that would help manage your diabetes?" These types of questions help the patient think about the benefits of managing their condition and how they can take control of their health.

Conclusion

Motivational Interviewing is a powerful tool that helps people explore their own reasons for change. By focusing on empathy, active listening, and collaboration, MI encourages individuals to resolve their ambivalence and take positive steps toward achieving their goals. Whether it's used in healthcare, counseling, coaching, education, or social work, MI offers a flexible, effective approach to guiding people through the process of change.

In each setting, the key to MI's success is its focus on empowering the individual to take charge of their own decisions. Instead of being told what to do, people are invited to explore their feelings, weigh their options, and discover why making a change is important to them. This makes MI a respectful, supportive, and highly effective way to foster meaningful and lasting behavior change.

Chapter 2: Core Principles of MI

Motivational Interviewing (MI) is grounded in four core principles that serve as the foundation for the entire approach. These principles—partnership, acceptance, compassion, and evocation—are designed to create a safe and supportive environment for change. By focusing on these principles, MI practitioners help individuals explore their own motivations for change in a way that feels respectful, non-judgmental, and empowering.

Let's dive deeper into each of these principles, exploring what they mean, how they work, and how they can be applied in real-life scenarios.

Partnership
What it means:
Partnership in Motivational Interviewing is all about collaboration. The idea is that the practitioner and the individual are working together as equals to explore the person's goals and motivations. Instead of taking on the role of an "expert" who gives advice or solutions, the practitioner engages the person in a conversation where both parties contribute equally. The practitioner brings their skills in guiding the conversation, and the individual brings their own knowledge of their life, challenges, and aspirations.

In partnership, the practitioner doesn't try to "fix" the person or tell them what to do. Instead, they join with the individual to explore possibilities for change. This approach helps to build trust and rapport because the person feels like they are being listened to and respected.

Real-life example:
Imagine a nutritionist working with a client who wants to lose weight. Instead of telling the client what foods they should or shouldn't eat, the nutritionist approaches the conversation as a partnership. They might ask, "What are some of your favorite healthy foods?" or "How do you feel about making small changes to your meals?" By asking these kinds of open-ended questions, the nutritionist allows the client to take part in the decision-making process, making the client feel more empowered and in control.

How it creates a supportive environment for change:
Partnership helps create a safe and supportive environment by ensuring that the individual feels heard and respected. When people feel like they are part of the process, they are more likely to engage and take ownership of their decisions. This collaborative approach encourages self-confidence and reduces resistance to change because the individual doesn't feel like they are being pushed into something they're not ready for.

Another example in healthcare:
Consider a doctor working with a patient who has high blood pressure. The patient is hesitant to start medication and isn't sure about making lifestyle changes. Instead of insisting on one approach, the doctor could say, "Let's work together to find a plan that feels manageable for you. What are some changes you think you could try?" This kind

of partnership fosters a sense of shared responsibility and encourages the patient to actively participate in their care.

Acceptance
What it means:
Acceptance in MI means embracing the individual as they are, without judgment or criticism. It's about creating an environment where the person feels valued and understood, no matter where they are in their journey. Acceptance has four key components: absolute worth, accurate empathy, autonomy, and affirmation.

- **Absolute worth** means recognizing the inherent value of each person. Everyone deserves respect and dignity, regardless of their behavior or situation.

- **Accurate empathy** involves listening deeply and understanding the person's feelings and perspective without trying to fix or change them.

- **Autonomy** refers to acknowledging that the individual has the right to make their own decisions, even if those decisions might not align with what others think is best.

- **Affirmation** is about recognizing and celebrating the person's strengths and efforts, no matter how small.

Real-life example:
A counselor working with a teenager who is struggling with school might use the principle of acceptance by

acknowledging the teen's feelings and experiences. Instead of focusing on what the teenager "should" be doing, the counselor might say, "It sounds like you've been feeling really overwhelmed lately. That makes sense, considering how much pressure you're under." This kind of statement shows that the counselor is accepting the teen's perspective and emotions, which helps to build trust.

How it creates a supportive environment for change:
Acceptance creates a safe space where people feel comfortable exploring their thoughts and feelings without fear of being judged. When individuals feel accepted, they are more likely to open up and share their true feelings, which is crucial for making lasting change. Acceptance also reinforces the idea that the person is in control of their own decisions, which helps to reduce defensiveness and resistance.

Another example in addiction treatment:
In a session with a client who is struggling with alcohol use, a therapist might say, "I can see that quitting drinking feels really challenging for you right now, and that's completely understandable." This simple statement conveys acceptance of the client's feelings and acknowledges the difficulty of the situation without passing judgment. The client is likely to feel supported and understood, which makes them more open to discussing their options for change.

Compassion
What it means:
Compassion in MI is about having a genuine desire to help the individual improve their well-being. It goes beyond sympathy or empathy by actively focusing on the person's needs and offering support in a way that is non-judgmental and caring. Compassion means putting the other person's interests first, rather than focusing on what the practitioner thinks is best.

In MI, compassion involves understanding the person's struggles and challenges while also holding hope and belief in their capacity to change. The practitioner shows that they truly care about the individual's well-being, which helps to build a strong, trusting relationship.

Real-life example:
A life coach working with a client who wants to make a career change might show compassion by acknowledging how difficult it is to leave a stable job, even if the client is unhappy. The coach could say, "I know this is a big decision, and it's really brave of you to even consider making a change. It shows that you care about your future and your happiness." This kind of compassionate response helps the client feel supported and encourages them to take the next step.

How it creates a supportive environment for change:
Compassion fosters a deep sense of trust between the practitioner and the individual. When people feel that someone genuinely cares about their well-being, they are more likely to be open, honest, and willing to explore their options. Compassion also reduces fear and anxiety about

making changes, as the person knows they will be supported no matter what choices they make.

Another example in mental health counseling:
In a counseling session, a therapist might show compassion to a client who is dealing with depression by saying, "I can see how much you've been struggling, and it's clear that you're doing the best you can right now. It's okay to take things one step at a time." This compassionate response reassures the client that they don't need to rush or be perfect, which helps to reduce feelings of pressure and overwhelm.

Evocation
What it means:
Evocation is the principle that change comes from within the individual, not from outside pressure or advice. In MI, the practitioner's role is to "evoke" or draw out the person's own motivations, strengths, and desires for change. Instead of telling the person what they should do, the practitioner helps them discover their own reasons for wanting to change.

Evocation is based on the idea that people already have the resources they need to make changes—they just need help accessing them. The practitioner uses open-ended questions, reflective listening, and other techniques to guide the individual in exploring their own motivations and developing a plan for change.

Real-life example:
A fitness coach working with a client who wants to start

exercising might use evocation by asking, "What would it mean to you to feel stronger and more energetic?" or "How do you think your life would change if you made exercise a regular part of your routine?" These questions help the client reflect on their own reasons for wanting to exercise, rather than focusing on external pressures or expectations.

How it creates a supportive environment for change:
Evocation empowers individuals by showing them that they have the ability to make their own decisions and take control of their own lives. When people are able to articulate their own reasons for change, they are more likely to feel motivated and committed to the process. Evocation also reduces resistance because the individual isn't being told what to do—they are discovering their own path forward.

Another example in smoking cessation:
A nurse working with a patient who is trying to quit smoking might ask, "What are some reasons you've thought about quitting?" and "How would quitting smoking improve your life?" These questions encourage the patient to reflect on their own motivations, such as improving their health or setting a good example for their children. By evoking the patient's own reasons for change, the nurse helps them feel more motivated and confident in their ability to quit.

How These Principles Work Together to Create a Safe and Supportive Environment for Change

When used together, the four core principles of Motivational Interviewing—partnership, acceptance, compassion, and evocation—create an environment that feels safe, supportive, and empowering. This environment is crucial for helping individuals explore their ambivalence, build motivation, and make meaningful changes in their lives.

1. **Partnership** ensures that the individual feels like an equal partner in the process. They are not being told what to do or pushed in a certain direction. Instead, they are working collaboratively with the practitioner to explore their options and make decisions that feel right for them.

2. **Acceptance** creates a non-judgmental space where the individual feels valued and understood. When people feel accepted for who they are, they are more likely to be open and honest about their thoughts, feelings, and challenges.

3. **Compassion** shows the individual that the practitioner genuinely cares about their well-being. This helps to build trust and reduces anxiety about making changes. People are more likely to feel motivated and supported when they know that someone truly cares about their success.

4. **Evocation** empowers the individual to take control of their own change process. By drawing out the person's own motivations and strengths, the practitioner helps them feel confident and capable of making positive changes.

Together, these principles create a foundation for Motivational Interviewing that is respectful, empathetic, and focused on the individual's needs and goals. This approach makes it easier for people to overcome ambivalence, build motivation, and take meaningful steps toward lasting change.

Chapter 3: The Spirit of MI

Motivational Interviewing (MI) is more than just a set of techniques or a checklist of things to do in a conversation. At its core, MI is guided by a particular "spirit" or way of being with people. This spirit is what makes MI unique and effective in helping individuals explore their feelings and motivations for change. In this chapter, we'll dive into the key elements that define the spirit of MI, including empathy, active listening, and collaboration. We'll also explore how ambivalence plays a central role in the decision-making process and how MI helps people navigate it.

Understanding Empathy, Active Listening, and Collaboration

At the heart of MI lies the spirit of understanding and working together with the person you're trying to help. Let's break down these three key concepts:

Empathy
What is empathy?

Empathy is the ability to understand and share the feelings of another person. In the context of MI, empathy goes beyond simply acknowledging what someone is going through—it's about really getting inside their perspective and seeing the world through their eyes. It's feeling with the person, not just feeling for them.

Imagine you're talking to a friend who is feeling overwhelmed by work. Instead of just saying, "I'm sorry to hear that," empathy involves saying something like, "That sounds really tough, I can imagine it must feel like everything is piling up on you." By reflecting their experience back to them, you're showing that you not only hear what they're saying but also understand how they feel.

In MI, empathy is key to building a strong, trusting relationship with the person. When they feel like you truly understand them, they're more likely to open up and explore their feelings about change.

Real-life example:

Let's say a healthcare professional is working with a patient who has been struggling to stick to their diabetes management plan. The patient feels frustrated and guilty because they haven't been following their doctor's recommendations. Instead of lecturing the patient or telling them what they "should" be doing, the healthcare provider uses empathy. They might say, "It sounds like you've been feeling overwhelmed by all the changes you've been asked to make. Managing diabetes can be really tough, especially when it feels like it's taking over your life." By empathizing with the patient's feelings, the healthcare provider creates a safe space for the patient to talk openly about their struggles.

How empathy creates a supportive environment for change:

When people feel understood, they're more likely to let down their defenses and explore their feelings honestly. Empathy helps to build rapport and trust, which are essential for helping someone work through their ambivalence about change. By demonstrating empathy, the practitioner shows that they are on the person's side and that their feelings are valid.

Active Listening
What is active listening?

Active listening is more than just hearing the words that someone is saying—it's about paying full attention to the person and engaging with their message on a deeper level. In MI, active listening involves listening for the meaning behind the words, as well as paying attention to the person's emotions, body language, and tone of voice.

Active listening means giving the person your full attention, without interrupting, judging, or thinking about what you're going to say next. It also involves using reflective statements to show that you're really tuned in to what the person is saying.

For example, if someone says, "I've been trying to quit smoking, but it's so hard because I'm stressed all the time," an active listener might respond with, "It sounds like stress is making it really difficult for you to stop smoking right now." This type of response shows that you're not only listening but also understanding the emotions and struggles behind the person's words.

Real-life example:

A counselor working with a teenager who is struggling with school might use active listening to help the teen feel heard. The teenager might say, "I don't see the point of trying anymore. No matter how hard I work, I still fail." Instead of jumping in with advice or trying to fix the problem, the counselor could respond with, "It sounds like you're feeling really discouraged and frustrated with school." By actively listening and reflecting the teen's feelings back to them, the counselor creates a space for the teen to explore their emotions without feeling judged or dismissed.

How active listening creates a supportive environment for change:

Active listening helps people feel valued and understood. It shows that you're fully present in the conversation and that you care about what the person is saying. When people feel like they're being listened to, they're more likely to open up and share their thoughts and feelings, which is crucial for working through ambivalence and making positive changes.

Collaboration
What is collaboration?

Collaboration in MI means working together with the person as a team. It's not about being the expert who tells the person what to do—it's about partnering with them to explore their goals, challenges, and motivations. In a collaborative relationship, the person is seen as the expert on their own life, and the practitioner is there to help guide the conversation and offer support.

Collaboration is about empowering the person to take control of their own change process. Instead of giving advice or making decisions for them, the practitioner helps the person explore their options and make choices that align with their values and goals.

Real-life example:

Imagine a life coach working with a client who wants to improve their work-life balance. Instead of giving the client a list of things they should do, the coach uses a collaborative approach. They might say, "Let's work together to come up with a plan that feels manageable for you. What are some changes you think you could start with?" By collaborating with the client, the coach empowers them to take ownership of their decisions and feel more invested in the process.

How collaboration creates a supportive environment for change:

Collaboration fosters a sense of shared responsibility and empowerment. When people feel like they're part of the decision-making process, they're more likely to feel motivated and confident in their ability to make changes. Collaboration also reduces resistance because the person doesn't feel like they're being told what to do—they're actively involved in shaping their own path.

The Role of Ambivalence in Decision-Making

Ambivalence is a key concept in MI and plays a central role in the decision-making process. Ambivalence means having mixed or contradictory feelings about something. It's that "push-pull" feeling you get when you know you should do something, but part of you doesn't want to.

In the context of change, ambivalence is very common. People often feel torn between wanting to make a positive change (like quitting smoking, losing weight, or improving their relationships) and feeling unsure or hesitant about it. This inner conflict can make it hard for people to take action, even when they know that change would be good for them.

Let's explore the role of ambivalence in decision-making and how MI helps people navigate this challenging process.

Understanding Ambivalence
What is ambivalence?

Ambivalence is the feeling of being stuck between two opposing desires or motivations. It's like being caught in a tug-of-war between wanting to make a change and wanting to stay the same. For example, someone might want to quit drinking because they know it's bad for their health, but at the same time, they enjoy the social aspect of drinking and aren't sure if they're ready to give it up.

Ambivalence is a natural part of the change process. It's not a sign that the person is unmotivated or lazy—it's simply a reflection of the complexity of human behavior. People often have both positive and negative feelings about change, and these conflicting emotions can make it difficult to move forward.

Real-life example:

Let's say a person is trying to decide whether to start exercising regularly. On one hand, they know that exercise will help them feel healthier, have more energy, and reduce stress. But on the other hand, they're worried about the time commitment and whether they'll be able to stick with it. This person is experiencing ambivalence—they can see the benefits of exercising, but they also have doubts and concerns.

How ambivalence affects decision-making:

Ambivalence can make decision-making feel overwhelming. When people are torn between two options, they may feel paralyzed and unable to take action. They might go back and forth, weighing the pros and cons, without ever making a decision. This indecision can lead to frustration and feelings of being stuck.

Ambivalence can also lead to resistance. If someone feels pressured to make a change before they're ready, they may push back or dig in their heels, even if they know that the change would be beneficial. For example, if a person feels pressured to quit smoking by their family or friends, they might become defensive and resist making a decision, even if part of them wants to quit.

How MI Helps People Navigate Ambivalence

In MI, the goal is not to "fix" ambivalence or force the person to make a decision. Instead, MI helps people explore their ambivalence in a safe and supportive way, allowing them to resolve their inner conflict and move toward change at their own pace.

Here are some key ways MI helps people navigate ambivalence:

---

1. Exploring Both Sides of Ambivalence

One of the most important things MI does is help people explore both sides of their ambivalence. Instead of focusing only on the reasons for change, MI encourages people to talk about their reasons for staying the same. By acknowledging both sides of the ambivalence, the practitioner helps the person understand their inner conflict more clearly.

Real-life example:

A counselor working with a client who is considering quitting smoking might say, "It sounds like part of you really wants to quit smoking because you're worried about your health, but another part of you isn't sure because smoking helps you relax when you're stressed. Can you tell me more about both of those feelings?" By inviting the client to explore both sides of their ambivalence, the counselor helps them gain a deeper understanding of their conflicting emotions.

2. Reflective Listening

Reflective listening is a key technique in MI that helps people feel heard and understood. When someone expresses ambivalence, the practitioner reflects back what they're hearing in a non-judgmental way. This helps the person feel validated and encourages them to continue exploring their feelings.

Real-life example:

A person might say, "I know I should probably start eating healthier, but I really love fast food, and I'm not sure if I'm ready to give it up." A practitioner using MI might respond with a reflective statement like, "It sounds like you're feeling torn between wanting to make healthier choices and not wanting to give up something you enjoy." This type of reflection helps the person feel understood and encourages them to keep talking about their ambivalence.

3. Eliciting "Change Talk"

In MI, "change talk" refers to statements that indicate a desire, ability, or willingness to change. One of the key goals of MI is to help people move from ambivalence to change by encouraging more "change talk." This is done by asking open-ended questions, using reflective listening, and affirming the person's strengths and motivations.

Real-life example:

A person who is ambivalent about losing weight might say, "I know I should probably start exercising, but I just don't have the time." A practitioner using MI might respond with, "It sounds like time is a big challenge for you, but it also sounds like you've been thinking about the benefits of exercise. What would it look like if you found a small way to fit exercise into your day?" This type of question helps the person start thinking about possible solutions, which can lead to more "change talk" as they begin to explore their options.

4. Supporting Autonomy

In MI, it's essential to support the person's autonomy—their right to make their own decisions. When people feel like they are in control of the change process, they are more likely to feel motivated and less resistant. Instead of pressuring the person to make a change, MI helps them explore their options and make decisions that align with their values and goals.

Real-life example:

A doctor working with a patient who is considering cutting back on alcohol might say, "It's completely up to you whether or not you want to make any changes right now. What do you think would be the first step if you decided to cut back?" By supporting the patient's autonomy, the doctor empowers them to take control of their own change process.

Conclusion: How the Spirit of MI and Ambivalence Work Together

The spirit of MI—empathy, active listening, and collaboration—creates a supportive and empowering environment for people to explore their ambivalence and make decisions about change. Ambivalence is a natural part of the change process, and MI helps people navigate it by encouraging open exploration of their conflicting feelings. By using techniques like reflective listening, eliciting change talk, and supporting autonomy, MI practitioners help people resolve their ambivalence and move toward positive change at their own pace.

This compassionate, person-centered approach is what makes MI so effective in helping individuals take control of their own lives and make meaningful, lasting changes.

Chapter 4: The Four Processes of MI

Motivational Interviewing (MI) is a client-centered approach to communication that helps people explore and resolve their ambivalence about making changes in their lives. MI is structured around four key processes that guide conversations and help individuals move from uncertainty about change to taking meaningful action. These four processes are:

1. **Engaging**: Building rapport and trust
2. **Focusing**: Narrowing the conversation to a specific goal
3. **Evoking**: Drawing out the person's own motivations for change
4. **Planning**: Helping clients commit to actionable steps

In this comprehensive explanation, we will explore each of these four processes in detail, provide real-life examples, and explain how they work together to help people make positive changes.

Engaging
Building Rapport and Trust

What is Engaging?

Engaging is the foundation of MI and involves building a relationship of trust and rapport with the person you are working with. Without engagement, it's difficult to move forward with the conversation because the person may feel guarded, defensive, or uninterested in exploring change.

Engaging is all about creating a safe, non-judgmental space where the person feels heard, understood, and respected. It involves active listening, empathy, and showing genuine interest in the person's thoughts, feelings, and experiences. The goal of engaging is to establish a connection that allows for open and honest communication.

Key elements of engaging:

- Listening more than talking
- Asking open-ended questions
- Reflecting back what the person says to show understanding
- Demonstrating empathy and acceptance
- Avoiding judgment, criticism, or advice-giving early in the conversation

Real-life example:

Imagine a counselor working with a client who is considering quitting smoking. The client might come into the conversation feeling unsure or resistant about discussing their smoking habits. The counselor's first task is to engage the client by creating a space where they feel comfortable sharing their thoughts.

Instead of immediately asking the client about their smoking, the counselor might start by asking more general questions to get to know the client better. They could ask, "What does a typical day look like for you?" or "What are some things that are going well in your life right now?" By starting with open-ended questions and showing interest in the client as a whole person, the counselor helps build rapport and trust.

How engaging creates a foundation for change:

When people feel engaged and connected in a conversation, they are more likely to open up about their thoughts and feelings, including their ambivalence about change. Building trust allows the person to feel safe enough to explore their motivations, challenges, and goals. Without engagement, it's difficult to move forward in the MI process because the person may not feel comfortable discussing sensitive or personal issues.

Focusing
What is Focusing?

Focusing is the process of narrowing the conversation to a specific change goal or area of concern. Once rapport and trust have been established during the engaging process, the conversation can shift toward identifying the issue or behavior that the person wants to work on. Focusing helps both the practitioner and the individual clarify the direction of the conversation and agree on a common goal.

In MI, focusing is done collaboratively. The practitioner doesn't impose a goal on the person; instead, they work together to identify an area of focus that feels important and meaningful to the individual. Focusing helps to bring clarity and structure to the conversation, making it easier to explore the person's motivations and develop a plan for change.

Key elements of focusing:

- Identifying the person's priorities and goals
- Exploring the individual's values and what matters most to them
- Clarifying the specific behavior or issue the person wants to address
- Working together to agree on a focus for the conversation

Real-life example:

Let's say a social worker is working with a client who has been struggling with multiple challenges, including financial stress, relationship issues, and health concerns. During the engaging process, the social worker has learned about these different areas of the client's life. Now it's time to focus the conversation on one specific area.

The social worker might say, "It sounds like there's a lot going on for you right now. Of all the things we've talked about, is there one area that feels most important for us to focus on today?" The client might respond by saying, "I think I really need to work on my finances. I'm falling behind on bills, and it's causing a lot of stress." By collaboratively identifying a specific focus—managing financial stress—the social worker and client can begin to work toward a concrete goal.

How focusing helps create clarity and direction:

Focusing helps to clarify the direction of the conversation and ensures that both the practitioner and the individual are on the same page. By narrowing the conversation to a specific goal, the person can begin to explore their thoughts, feelings, and motivations related to that goal. Focusing also prevents the conversation from becoming too broad or overwhelming, which can make it difficult for the person to move forward.

Evoking
Drawing Out the Person's Own Motivations for Change

What is Evoking?

Evoking is the heart of MI and involves drawing out the person's own motivations, reasons, and desires for change. In MI, it's not about telling the person what they should do or why they should change; instead, it's about helping them discover their own motivations for change. People are more likely to make lasting changes when they are guided to identify their own reasons for wanting to change, rather than being told by someone else.

Evoking is often achieved by asking open-ended questions that encourage the person to reflect on their values, goals, and desires. It also involves listening for "change talk," which are statements that indicate the person is considering or leaning toward change. The practitioner uses reflective listening to highlight and reinforce the person's change talk, helping them build momentum toward making a decision.

Key elements of evoking:

- Asking open-ended questions that encourage self-reflection
- Listening for and reinforcing "change talk"
- Exploring the person's values, goals, and reasons for change
- Avoiding giving advice or trying to "convince" the person to change

Real-life example:

A healthcare provider is working with a patient who has been struggling with high blood pressure. The patient knows that they should reduce their salt intake and exercise more, but they haven't made any changes yet. Instead of lecturing the patient about the dangers of high blood pressure, the healthcare provider uses evoking to help the patient explore their own reasons for change.

The provider might ask, "What would it mean for you to have better control over your blood pressure?" or "How do you think your life would be different if you started making some small changes to your diet and exercise routine?" These open-ended questions encourage the patient to think about the positive outcomes of change, such as feeling healthier, having more energy, or reducing their risk of complications.

As the patient begins to talk about the benefits of change, the provider listens for change talk. The patient might say, "I know I'd feel better if I exercised more," or "I want to be around for my grandkids, so I know I need to take better care of myself." The provider reflects these statements back to the patient, reinforcing their motivation for change: "It sounds like being there for your grandkids is really important to you, and you see how taking care of your health can help make that happen."

How evoking helps build motivation:

Evoking helps people connect with their own reasons for change, which increases their motivation and commitment. When individuals are guided to articulate their own desires for change, they are more likely to feel ownership over the process and become more invested in making it happen. Evoking also helps to resolve ambivalence by focusing on the person's intrinsic motivations rather than external pressures.

Planning
Helping Clients Commit to Actionable Steps

What is Planning?

Planning is the final process in MI and involves helping the person move from contemplation to action. Once the person has explored their motivations for change and feels ready to take the next step, the practitioner works with them to develop a concrete, actionable plan. Planning is about turning intentions into action by helping the person identify specific steps they can take to achieve their goals.

In MI, planning is done collaboratively, just like the other processes. The practitioner helps the person brainstorm ideas, explore potential obstacles, and identify strategies for success. The goal is to create a plan that feels realistic, achievable, and aligned with the person's values and priorities.

Key elements of planning:

- Helping the person identify specific, actionable steps they can take
- Exploring potential challenges or barriers to change
- Supporting the person in developing a plan that feels realistic and achievable
- Reinforcing the person's confidence and commitment to their plan

Real-life example:

A fitness coach is working with a client who has expressed a desire to start exercising regularly. During the evoking process, the client has identified their motivation for change—they want to have more energy and improve their overall health. Now, the coach helps the client move into the planning phase by developing a specific exercise plan.

The coach might ask, "What's one small step you could take this week to get started with your exercise routine?" The client might respond, "I think I could start by going for a 20-minute walk after dinner a couple of times a week." The coach then helps the client think through the logistics of their plan: "That sounds like a great start. Do you think there are any challenges that might get in the way of doing that?" The client might mention that they sometimes feel tired after work, so the coach helps them come up with a strategy for staying motivated, such as setting a reminder on their phone or inviting a friend to join them on the walk.

How planning helps turn intentions into action:

Planning helps individuals move from thinking about change to actually taking action. By developing a clear, actionable plan, the person feels more confident and prepared to make the changes they've been considering. Planning also helps to address potential obstacles before they arise, which increases the likelihood of success. When people have a plan that feels realistic and achievable, they are more likely to follow through and make meaningful progress toward their goals.

How the Four Processes Work Together

The four processes of MI—engaging, focusing, evoking, and planning—are designed to work together in a flexible, client-centered way. Each process builds on the one before it, helping to guide the person through the stages of change. Here's how they work together:

1. **Engaging** lays the foundation by building rapport and trust. Without engagement, the conversation can't move forward effectively.

2. **Focusing** narrows the conversation to a specific goal or behavior that the person wants to work on, providing clarity and direction.

3. **Evoking** helps the person explore their own motivations for change, building the internal desire and commitment to take action.

4. **Planning** turns that motivation into action by developing a concrete, realistic plan for change.

By following these four processes, practitioners can help individuals move from ambivalence and uncertainty to motivation and action. MI's focus on collaboration, empathy, and respect empowers people to take control of their own change process, making it more likely that the changes they make will be meaningful and lasting.

Conclusion

The four processes of MI provide a structured yet flexible framework for helping people navigate the complexities of change. Whether you're working with someone who is struggling with addiction, trying to improve their health, or looking to make positive life changes, MI offers a powerful, person-centered approach that supports individuals in making decisions that align with their values and goals. Through engaging, focusing, evoking, and planning, MI helps people move from uncertainty to action, empowering them to make meaningful and lasting changes in their lives.

Chapter 5: The OARS Model of MI

Motivational Interviewing (MI) is a client-centered, goal-oriented approach that focuses on exploring and resolving ambivalence to facilitate change. One of the core communication techniques within MI is the OARS model, which stands for:

1. **Open-ended questions**
2. **Affirmations**
3. **Reflective listening**
4. **Summarizing**

The OARS model provides practitioners with a simple but powerful set of tools to facilitate productive conversations. Whether you're working in healthcare, counseling, education, or even coaching, the OARS techniques can help you engage with people in a meaningful way, making it easier to guide them toward change.

This comprehensive explanation will dive into each element of the OARS model, provide real-life examples, and offer practical exercises for beginners to practice and master these essential skills.

Open-ended Questions
What are open-ended questions?

Open-ended questions are questions that cannot be answered with a simple "yes" or "no." Instead, they encourage the person to think more deeply and provide more detailed responses. Open-ended questions help to open up the conversation and allow the individual to explore their thoughts, feelings, and motivations.

Open-ended questions typically start with words like "what," "how," or "tell me about." These types of questions encourage the person to reflect on their experiences and give more expansive answers. In MI, open-ended questions are used to help people explore their ambivalence about change, identify their values, and think about possible solutions.

Real-life examples of open-ended questions:

- Instead of asking, "Do you want to quit smoking?" (which could be answered with a simple "yes" or "no"), you might ask, "What are some of the reasons you've been thinking about quitting smoking?"

- Instead of asking, "Are you happy with your progress?" you might ask, "How do you feel about the progress you've made so far?"

How open-ended questions promote change:

Open-ended questions allow the person to explore their feelings in a more open and honest way. By encouraging the individual to talk more freely, the practitioner can gain a deeper understanding of their motivations, concerns, and goals. This helps create a collaborative, non-judgmental atmosphere where the person feels comfortable exploring their ambivalence and considering different options for change.

Practical exercises for practicing open-ended questions:

- **Exercise 1: Rewriting Closed-ended Questions**
  Take a list of common closed-ended questions and practice converting them into open-ended questions. For example:
    - Closed: "Do you think you need to exercise more?"
    - Open: "What are your thoughts about getting more exercise?"

Practice rewriting closed-ended questions into open-ended versions to encourage deeper conversation.

- **Exercise 2: Open-ended Question Journal**
  Keep a journal where you write down five open-ended questions each day. These questions can be related to different aspects of life, such as health, relationships, or career. Over time, this will help you develop the habit of asking open-ended questions naturally.

Affirmations
What are affirmations?

Affirmations are positive statements that recognize and acknowledge a person's strengths, efforts, or values. In MI, affirmations are used to reinforce the individual's confidence and self-efficacy. They focus on the person's abilities and what they're doing right, rather than what they're doing wrong.

Affirmations help to build a supportive and encouraging atmosphere. When people feel recognized for their efforts, they are more likely to feel motivated and capable of making positive changes.

Key features of affirmations:

- They focus on strengths, efforts, or qualities.
- They are genuine and specific, rather than generic praise.
- They help build self-esteem and confidence.

Real-life examples of affirmations:

- "It's clear that you've been really committed to making progress, even though it's been tough at times."
- "You've shown a lot of determination by sticking with your plan, even when you were feeling discouraged."

How affirmations promote change:

Affirmations help people feel more confident in their ability to make changes. When someone hears positive feedback about their efforts or strengths, it reinforces their sense of self-worth and capability. This can be particularly helpful when the person is feeling uncertain or struggling with ambivalence. By focusing on what the person is doing well, affirmations create a positive atmosphere that encourages continued progress.

Practical exercises for practicing affirmations:

- **Exercise 1: Affirmation Bank**
  Make a list of positive affirmations that you can use in different situations. For example, affirmations related to effort, progress, or resilience. Practice incorporating these affirmations into your conversations with others.

- **Exercise 2: Affirmation Practice Role-Play**
  Pair up with a friend or colleague and practice giving each other affirmations. One person can talk about a personal challenge or goal, and the other person can respond with affirmations that acknowledge their strengths and efforts. After the role-play, discuss how the affirmations made you feel and how you can use them in real-life situations.

Reflective Listening
What is reflective listening?

Reflective listening is the practice of carefully listening to what someone is saying and then reflecting it back to them in your own words. The goal of reflective listening is to show the person that you are truly listening and understanding their thoughts and feelings. It also helps the individual to hear their own words reflected back, which can lead to new insights and a deeper understanding of their own motivations.

In MI, reflective listening is a key tool for helping people explore their ambivalence about change. By reflecting what the person says, you create a space where they can process their thoughts and feelings more fully.

Types of reflections:

- **Simple reflections**: Repeating or paraphrasing what the person has said.

- **Complex reflections**: Adding deeper meaning or insight to what the person has said.

Real-life examples of reflective listening:

- Person: "I know I need to eat healthier, but I just don't have the time to cook meals every day."
    - Simple reflection: "It sounds like you want to eat healthier but feel like time is a barrier for you."
    - Complex reflection: "It sounds like balancing your busy schedule with healthy eating has been a real challenge for you."

How reflective listening promotes change:

Reflective listening helps people feel heard and understood. When individuals feel that their thoughts and feelings are being taken seriously, they are more likely to open up and explore their ambivalence. Reflective listening also helps to deepen the conversation by encouraging the person to think more critically about their own statements. This can lead to new insights, which can help resolve ambivalence and build motivation for change.

Practical exercises for practicing reflective listening:

- **Exercise 1: Mirror Reflections**
  Practice reflecting what someone has said in your own words. During a conversation, listen carefully to what the other person says and then reflect it back to them. For example, if someone says, "I'm feeling really stressed about work," you might reflect, "It sounds like work has been a major source of stress for you lately." Practice this with friends, colleagues, or in everyday conversations.

- **Exercise 2: Listening Game**
  Pair up with someone and take turns speaking and reflecting. One person shares a story or experience, and the other person practices reflecting what they hear. After the reflection, the speaker can provide feedback on whether the reflection captured their feelings accurately. This exercise helps develop reflective listening skills in a fun and supportive way.

Summarizing
What is summarizing?

Summarizing involves pulling together key points from a conversation and reflecting them back to the person in a clear and concise way. Summaries help to organize and clarify what has been discussed, which can be particularly useful in longer or more complex conversations. Summarizing also provides an opportunity to reinforce the person's motivations and goals.

In MI, summarizing is used to gather the key themes of the conversation and highlight important points, such as the person's reasons for change, their ambivalence, and their strengths. Summaries help to bring the conversation to a close or transition to a new phase of the discussion.

Real-life examples of summarizing:

- "So, what I'm hearing is that you really want to be more active because you know it will help you feel better, but you're worried about finding the time to fit it into your schedule. Is that right?"
- "To summarize, you've talked about how important it is for you to quit smoking, especially because you want to set a good example for your kids. At the same time, you're feeling unsure about how to deal with stress without smoking."

How summarizing promotes change:

Summarizing helps people organize their thoughts and see the bigger picture. By pulling together the key points of the conversation, summaries help the person reflect on what they've discussed and how it relates to their goals. Summaries also reinforce important themes, such as the person's motivations, strengths, and challenges. This can help the person feel more focused and ready to take action.

Practical exercises for practicing summarizing:

- **Exercise 1: Summarizing Key Points**
  After a conversation or meeting, practice summarizing the key points in a few sentences. Focus on capturing the main themes and important details. You can also practice summarizing written material, such as articles or book chapters, to develop your summarizing skills.

- **Exercise 2: Conversation Summaries**
  Pair up with a friend or colleague and have a conversation about a particular topic. After the conversation, practice summarizing what was discussed by highlighting the key points. The other person can provide feedback on whether the summary captured the main ideas accurately.

Practical Exercises for Practicing OARS

Now that we've gone over the four elements of the OARS model—**Open-ended questions, Affirmations, Reflective listening,** and **Summarizing**—let's explore some practical exercises that can help beginners master these essential skills. Each exercise is designed to build your confidence and fluency with these techniques in real-world conversations.

---

1. Practicing Open-ended Questions

Objective:
To become comfortable asking open-ended questions that encourage deeper conversation and self-reflection.

Exercise 1: Reframing Closed Questions

Take common closed-ended questions and reframe them as open-ended questions. Here are a few examples to practice:

- **Closed question:** "Do you want to exercise more?"
    - **Reframe:** "What are your thoughts on incorporating more exercise into your daily routine?"
- **Closed question:** "Are you happy with your job?"
    - **Reframe:** "What do you enjoy about your current job, and what would you like to change?"
- **Closed question:** "Do you plan to quit smoking?"
    - **Reframe:** "What are some of the reasons you've been considering quitting smoking?"

Practice tip:
Write out 10 closed-ended questions, then reframe each one as an open-ended question. Use this exercise regularly to train your brain to think in open-ended terms.

Exercise 2: The "Why, What, How" Practice

For any given scenario or problem, try asking a question that starts with "Why," "What," or "How." These types of questions naturally open up the conversation. Here's how you can practice:

- **Scenario:** A client mentions they want to improve their diet but are struggling to make changes.

- **Why question:** "Why do you think making dietary changes is important for you?"
- **What question:** "What do you think has been the biggest challenge in changing your eating habits?"
- **How question:** "How do you imagine your life would be different if you were able to stick to your healthy eating plan?"

---

2. Practicing Affirmations

Objective:
To reinforce positive behaviors and attributes by acknowledging and affirming the person's strengths, efforts, and progress.

Exercise 1: Affirmation Journaling

Each day, practice identifying and writing down affirmations about the people you interact with. Try to focus on specific actions or qualities you've noticed, such as effort, determination, or progress. For example:

- "You've shown a lot of resilience by sticking to your workout routine, even on the days you didn't feel like it."

- "It's impressive how you've managed to balance your work and family life despite the challenges you're facing."

After writing down the affirmations, reflect on how they might make the person feel if you were to say them aloud.

Exercise 2: Affirmation Practice with a Partner

Find a partner (a friend, family member, or colleague) and engage in a role-play exercise. Have them share a personal challenge or goal with you. Practice responding with affirmations that recognize their efforts and strengths. After the exercise, discuss how the affirmations made your partner feel.

Example:
Your partner says, "I've been trying to save money, but I keep slipping up and buying things I don't really need."

- Your affirmation might be: "It sounds like you're really trying hard to be mindful of your spending, and that's a big step forward."

---

3. Practicing Reflective Listening

Objective:
To listen actively and reflect back what the other person is saying, helping them feel heard and understood.

Exercise 1: Reflective Listening Role-play

Pair up with a friend or colleague and take turns speaking and reflecting. One person shares a personal story or experience, and the other practices reflective listening by paraphrasing or reflecting the speaker's thoughts and feelings.

- **Speaker's statement:** "I've been feeling really overwhelmed with work lately. No matter how much I try to get ahead, there's always something new that comes up."
- **Reflection:** "It sounds like you're feeling frustrated because, no matter how hard you work, it's difficult to stay on top of everything."

After the role-play, provide feedback to each other on whether the reflections captured the essence of the speaker's message.

Exercise 2: Listening for Emotion

During conversations with others, focus on listening for the emotions behind the words. Practice reflecting both the content and the emotional tone of what the person is saying.

Example:

- **Statement:** "I've been trying to stick to my diet, but I keep giving in to cravings."
- **Reflection:** "It sounds like you're frustrated with yourself for giving in, even though you're working hard to stick to your plan."

This practice helps you develop the ability to listen for deeper meanings and emotions, enhancing the quality of your reflective listening skills.

4. Practicing Summarizing

Objective:
To practice summarizing key points of a conversation concisely and effectively, reinforcing the individual's motivations and goals.

Exercise 1: Summarizing Conversations

After a conversation, practice summarizing the key points in a few sentences. Focus on capturing the main themes of what was discussed. For example:

- "So, from what you've shared, it sounds like you've been feeling really stressed about work, but you've also started thinking about how a daily routine could help you manage your time better. You've also mentioned that you're trying to find a balance between work and self-care."

Exercise 2: Summarizing Role-play

Pair up with someone and have a conversation about a particular topic, such as a personal goal or challenge. After the conversation, practice summarizing what was discussed. Be sure to include the person's motivations, concerns, and any steps they mentioned they might take.

For example, if the person talked about wanting to get more exercise, your summary might look like this:

- "You've shared that exercising more is really important to you because you want to improve your health and have more energy. You've also mentioned that time is a challenge, but you're thinking that starting with short walks a few times a week could be a good first step."

Using OARS in Real-Life Scenarios

Here are some scenarios where you can practice using all elements of the OARS model together:

Scenario 1: Helping Someone with Health Goals

Imagine you're working with someone who wants to start eating healthier and exercising more. Using OARS, you might approach the conversation like this:

- **Open-ended question:** "What are some of the reasons you want to focus on your health right now?"

- **Affirmation:** "It's great that you're really thinking about how to make your health a priority. That takes a lot of commitment."

- **Reflection:** "It sounds like you've been trying to get into healthier habits, but balancing work and family life has made it difficult."

- **Summary:** "So, it sounds like your main goal is to feel more energetic and improve your health, but you're worried about finding the time to make these changes. You've been thinking about starting with small steps, like cooking more at home and taking walks a few times a week."

Scenario 2: Supporting Career Change

Let's say someone is considering a career change but is unsure about making the leap. Using OARS, you might respond like this:

- **Open-ended question:** "What's been on your mind about making a career change?"

- **Affirmation:** "It sounds like you've given this a lot of thought, and it's impressive that you're really thinking about what's best for your future."

- **Reflection:** "It seems like you're excited about the idea of a new career, but you're also feeling a bit nervous about leaving the stability of your current job."

- **Summary:** "So, you've been weighing the pros and cons of making a change. You're feeling motivated to find something more fulfilling, but you also want to make sure you're making a stable, well-thought-out decision."

Integrating OARS into Everyday Conversations

The OARS model is not only useful for professional settings like counseling or coaching but can also be integrated into everyday conversations. Whether you're talking with friends, family members, or colleagues, using OARS can help you foster deeper, more meaningful interactions.

Everyday Example 1: Talking with a Friend about a New Project

Your friend is starting a new creative project, but they're feeling unsure about how to proceed.

- **Open-ended question:** "What excites you most about this project?"
- **Affirmation:** "You've always been really creative, and it's amazing that you're putting your ideas into action."
- **Reflection:** "It sounds like you're excited but also feeling a little overwhelmed with where to start."
- **Summary:** "So, you're really passionate about this project, but you're still figuring out the best way to begin. You've mentioned that breaking it down into smaller steps might help you get started."

Everyday Example 2: Supporting a Family Member

A family member is thinking about going back to school but is unsure if it's the right time.

- **Open-ended question:** "What's been motivating you to think about going back to school?"
- **Affirmation:** "It's inspiring that you're considering taking this step, even though it's a big decision."
- **Reflection:** "It sounds like you're really excited about learning new things, but you're also concerned about balancing school with your other responsibilities."
- **Summary:** "So, you're interested in going back to school because you love learning, but you're

thinking through how it will fit with the rest of your life right now."

Conclusion: Mastering the OARS Model

The OARS model is a foundational tool in Motivational Interviewing, and mastering it can enhance your ability to have productive, client-centered conversations. By using **open-ended questions**, **affirmations**, **reflective listening**, and **summarizing**, you can help individuals explore their motivations, build confidence, and move toward positive change.

The exercises provided in this guide will help you practice and refine your OARS skills. Over time, as you become more comfortable using these techniques, you'll find that they become a natural part of your communication style, helping you create supportive and collaborative conversations in both professional and personal contexts.

The key to mastering OARS is consistent practice. Whether you're engaging in role-play exercises, journaling, or using OARS in real-life scenarios, these skills will become second nature the more you use them. With time and practice, you'll be able to create meaningful, change-oriented conversations that truly help people move forward.

Chapter 6: Change Talk and Sustain Talk in MI

In Motivational Interviewing (MI), the conversation often revolves around two key types of language: **change talk** and **sustain talk**. These two types of talk reflect a person's ambivalence about making a change. Understanding, identifying, and responding to both change talk and sustain talk is essential in guiding individuals through the process of change.

This comprehensive explanation will explore what change talk and sustain talk are, how to identify and respond to them, and how to handle resistance that may arise during the conversation. We'll include multiple real-life examples to illustrate these concepts, making them easy to understand and apply.

What is Change Talk?
Change talk refers to any speech that indicates a person's desire, ability, reason, or commitment to make a change. It is the language that signals a person is considering, ready for, or moving toward change. In MI, recognizing and encouraging change talk is one of the most important skills a practitioner can develop because it helps move the person toward taking action.

Change talk can be subtle or explicit, and it typically falls into one of the following categories (DARN-C):

1. **Desire**: Statements about wanting to make a change. Example: "I'd like to be more active."

2. **Ability**: Statements about being able to make a change. Example: "I think I could start walking after work."

3. **Reasons**: Statements that provide reasons for making a change. Example: "I know it would be better for my health if I quit smoking."

4. **Need**: Statements expressing the need for change. Example: "I really need to start eating better."

5. **Commitment**: Statements indicating a person's commitment to making a change. Example: "I'm going to cut back on drinking starting next week."

Recognizing Change Talk

Recognizing change talk is about listening carefully to what the person is saying. It may not always be obvious, and sometimes it can be mixed in with sustain talk (which we'll discuss next). Here are some examples of change talk in real-life situations:

Example 1: Change Talk in Health
A person might say, "I know I need to lose weight. My doctor said it would help with my blood pressure, and I'm tired of feeling so sluggish."

This statement contains **desire** ("I know I need to lose weight"), **reasons** ("it would help with my blood pressure"), and **ability** ("I'm tired of feeling so sluggish," implying they want to feel better).

Example 2: Change Talk in Addiction
Someone struggling with alcohol might say, "I think I'm drinking too much. I can see it's affecting my relationships, and I don't like how I feel the next morning."

This statement includes **reasons** ("affecting my relationships") and **desire** ("I don't like how I feel").

What is Sustain Talk?
Sustain talk, on the other hand, represents the language a person uses to express their reasons for staying the same or maintaining the current behavior. It reflects the part of the person that is resistant to change and feels ambivalent about making any adjustments. Sustain talk often highlights barriers, fears, or justifications for not making a change.

Sustain talk can be understood as the person's argument for not changing, and it typically falls into similar categories as change talk:

1. **Desire**: Statements about wanting to stay the same. Example: "I really enjoy smoking. It helps me relax."

2. **Ability**: Statements about being unable to change. Example: "I don't think I can quit drinking. It's too hard."

3. **Reasons**: Statements that provide reasons for not changing. Example: "I don't have time to exercise. My schedule is too packed."

4. **Need**: Statements expressing the need to maintain the current behavior. Example: "I need to keep working long hours, even if it's stressful."

Recognizing Sustain Talk

Sustain talk can sometimes be more explicit than change talk, as it often reflects a person's reasons for not making a change. Here are some examples:

Example 1: Sustain Talk in Diet and Exercise
"I've tried to eat healthier before, but it never works. I don't have time to prepare meals, and I love fast food too much."

This statement includes **ability** ("it never works") and **reasons** ("I don't have time," "I love fast food").

Example 2: Sustain Talk in Addiction
"Quitting smoking would be too stressful right now. I've got too much going on, and smoking helps me cope."

This statement includes **need** ("I need smoking to cope") and **reasons** ("too much going on").

Identifying and Responding to Change Talk

Once you can identify change talk, the next step is to respond to it in a way that encourages and amplifies the person's motivations for change. This helps to strengthen their commitment and move them closer to taking action. Let's break down how to effectively respond to change talk.

Responding to Change Talk: OARS Techniques

The **OARS** skills (Open-ended questions, Affirmations, Reflective listening, and Summarizing) are essential for reinforcing change talk. Here's how each technique can be used:

1. **Open-ended Questions**
    - Open-ended questions encourage the person to elaborate on their change talk and explore it further. For example, if someone says, "I want to quit smoking," you might ask, "What makes quitting smoking important to you?"

2. **Affirmations**
    - Affirmations help build the person's confidence in their ability to change by acknowledging their strengths. If someone says, "I've been thinking about cutting back on drinking," you might respond, "It sounds like you've really put a lot of thought into making healthier choices."

3. **Reflective Listening**
    - Reflective listening involves reflecting back the person's change talk in a way that encourages them to continue talking about their desire for change. For example, if someone says, "I know I'd feel better if I exercised more," you could reflect, "It sounds like you've been thinking a lot about

how exercise could improve your well-being."

4. **Summarizing**
    - Summarizing helps to reinforce change talk by pulling together the person's key statements about change. For example, you might say, "So, from what you've shared, it sounds like you're really interested in improving your health, and you've already been thinking about some steps you can take, like exercising more and eating healthier. Does that sound right?"

Real-life Example: Responding to Change Talk

Scenario: A person is discussing their struggles with drinking alcohol.

Change Talk Statement: "I've been thinking that maybe it's time to cut back on drinking. I don't like how I feel in the mornings, and I'm worried it's affecting my work."

Response Using OARS:

- **Open-ended question:** "What would life look like for you if you cut back on drinking?"
- **Affirmation:** "It sounds like you're really starting to reflect on how drinking is affecting your health and your work."

- **Reflective listening:** "It sounds like feeling better in the mornings and being more focused at work are important to you."
- **Summarizing:** "So, it sounds like cutting back on drinking is something you're considering because you want to feel better physically and improve your focus at work. Did I get that right?"

This response helps reinforce the person's change talk by encouraging them to elaborate on their reasons for change while affirming their strengths and motivations.

Handling Resistance and Sustain Talk

Sustain talk often reflects a person's resistance to change, and it can be challenging to navigate. In MI, resistance isn't seen as a barrier to overcome forcefully. Instead, it's understood as a natural part of the change process that requires empathy and skillful handling.

Common Types of Sustain Talk and Resistance

1. **Desire to Stay the Same**

    - Example: "I really don't want to give up smoking. I enjoy it too much."
    - Response: Instead of arguing or trying to convince the person, use reflective listening to acknowledge their feelings. You might say, "It sounds like smoking is something you really enjoy, and the idea of giving it up feels like a big loss."

2. **Doubt in Ability to Change**
    - Example: "I don't think I can lose weight. I've tried before, and it never works."
    - Response: Reflect the person's doubt while gently offering encouragement. "It sounds like you've had some tough experiences trying to lose weight in the past. What do you think could be different this time?"

3. **Reasons for Not Changing**
    - Example: "I'm too busy to exercise. My schedule just won't allow it."
    - Response: Avoid pushing solutions. Instead, reflect and explore. "It sounds like you've got a lot on your plate right now, and finding time for exercise feels difficult. Can we explore what your schedule looks like and see if there's a way to fit something small in?"

Strategies for Handling Sustain Talk

1. **Roll with Resistance**
    - Instead of confronting or arguing with the person's sustain talk, MI encourages practitioners to "roll with resistance." This means accepting the person's perspective and using it as an opportunity to explore their ambivalence further. By not pushing

back, you allow the person to express their concerns, which often leads to a deeper conversation about change.

Example:
If someone says, "I don't think I can quit drinking right now. It's just too hard," you might respond, "It sounds like quitting feels overwhelming for you at the moment, especially with everything else you're managing."

This response acknowledges the person's feelings without judgment or pressure, helping to maintain rapport and keep the conversation open.

2. **Double-sided Reflections**
    - Double-sided reflections acknowledge both the sustain talk and the change talk, highlighting the person's ambivalence. This technique involves reflecting both sides of the person's internal conflict without taking sides or pushing an agenda.

Example:
A person says, "I know I should exercise, but I just don't have the energy after work."
You might respond with, "It sounds like you're really torn between wanting to exercise for your health and feeling too tired at the end of the day."

By reflecting both sides, you show that you understand the person's ambivalence and are not trying to push them in either direction.

3. **Eliciting Change Talk in Response to Sustain Talk**

- Sustain talk can provide an opportunity to elicit more change talk by asking open-ended questions that explore the person's motivations for change.

Example:

If someone says, "I don't think I have time to cook healthy meals," you could ask, "What would it look like if you did have more time? How might that change things for you?"

This question encourages the person to think about the benefits of change and may lead to more change talk.

4. **Emphasizing Autonomy**
    - One of the key principles of MI is supporting the person's autonomy, or their ability to make their own choices. When you encounter sustain talk, it can be helpful to remind the person that the decision to change is entirely up to them.

Example:

If someone says, "I'm not sure I'm ready to quit smoking," you might respond, "That's completely your decision. You're the only one who can decide when and if you're ready to quit."

This response reduces pressure and reinforces the idea that the person is in control of their own choices, which can help reduce resistance.

Real-life Example: Handling Sustain Talk

Scenario:
A person is discussing their struggles with exercise and how they feel too tired to work out after a long day at work.

Sustain Talk Statement:
"I know I should exercise, but I just don't have the energy after work. I'm always too tired, and I don't see how I can fit it in."

Response Using MI Techniques:

- **Double-sided reflection:** "It sounds like you really value your health and want to exercise, but at the same time, you're feeling too exhausted after work to make it happen."

- **Open-ended question:** "What might make it easier for you to fit some physical activity into your day?"

- **Affirmation:** "It's great that you're thinking about ways to improve your health, even with all the challenges you're facing."

- **Emphasizing autonomy:** "Ultimately, it's your decision how and when to start making changes. What feels manageable for you right now?"

This response acknowledges the person's sustain talk (feeling tired and lacking time) while also gently encouraging them to think about possible solutions and reinforcing their control over the decision.

Conclusion: Balancing Change Talk and Sustain Talk in MI

Change talk and sustain talk are central components of any conversation about change. In Motivational Interviewing, the goal is not to eliminate sustain talk but to understand it as a natural part of the ambivalence people experience when considering change. By learning to identify and respond to both change talk and sustain talk, you can help people explore their own motivations, resolve their ambivalence, and move toward making meaningful changes in their lives.

Remember, change doesn't happen all at once. People often need time to work through their mixed feelings, and your role as a practitioner is to support them through that process with empathy, respect, and skillful communication. By using the techniques outlined here, you can create a safe, supportive environment where change talk is amplified, and sustain talk is understood and explored without judgment.

Chapter 7: Developing a Change Plan

Moving from Motivation to Action and Creating a Collaborative Change Plan

Developing a change plan is one of the most critical steps in helping individuals move from thinking about change to taking real, actionable steps toward achieving their goals. In Motivational Interviewing (MI), the process of developing a change plan is collaborative and centered around the individual's needs, values, and readiness. The plan is not something that is imposed by a counselor, coach, or healthcare provider but something that is co-created with the person to ensure that it is realistic, meaningful, and achievable.

In this comprehensive explanation, we'll walk through the process of moving from motivation to action, how to create a collaborative change plan, and include multiple real-life examples to illustrate these concepts in an easy-to-understand way.

Moving from Motivation to Action

Understanding that motivation is not the same as action is essential. People may feel motivated to change but still struggle to take the necessary steps to make that change a reality. Bridging the gap between motivation and action involves helping the person clarify their goals, identify barriers, and create a plan that includes specific steps toward change.

Why Motivation Isn't Enough

Motivation is an internal desire to make a change, but it doesn't automatically lead to action. People often feel motivated to improve their lives in some way, whether it's getting healthier, improving relationships, or managing stress. However, there are often obstacles that prevent them from moving forward, such as:

- Lack of clear goals
- Fear of failure
- Feeling overwhelmed by the process of change
- Not knowing where to start
- Competing priorities

MI helps address these barriers by encouraging individuals to reflect on their motivations, identify specific changes they want to make, and develop a plan that outlines the steps they will take.

Real-Life Example 1: From Motivation to Action in Health and Wellness

Scenario:
Sarah is a 40-year-old woman who wants to lose weight and improve her overall health. She feels motivated to make a change because her doctor has told her that losing weight will reduce her risk of heart disease. However, despite her motivation, Sarah hasn't made any concrete

steps toward improving her diet or starting an exercise routine.

Moving from Motivation to Action:

- **Clarifying the Goal:** The first step in moving Sarah from motivation to action is to help her clarify what she wants to achieve. Instead of focusing on a vague goal like "lose weight," Sarah needs to define what success looks like for her. The counselor might ask, "What specific changes would you like to make to your health?" Sarah responds, "I want to lose 20 pounds and have more energy."

- **Exploring Barriers:** Next, the counselor helps Sarah explore what's been holding her back. Sarah admits that she feels overwhelmed by the idea of overhauling her entire lifestyle. The counselor might respond, "It sounds like the idea of making big changes feels daunting. What do you think might be a manageable first step?" Sarah replies, "I think I could start by walking for 20 minutes a day."

- **Creating a First Step:** Once Sarah has identified a manageable first step, the counselor can help her think through how to turn that motivation into action. Sarah decides to start by walking every day after dinner for 20 minutes, and she feels confident that this is something she can stick to.

In this example, Sarah's motivation (wanting to improve her health) is turned into a concrete, actionable plan (walking for 20 minutes a day). The counselor helps Sarah break down her goal into smaller, more achievable steps, which helps her feel less overwhelmed and more capable of taking action.

Real-Life Example 2: From Motivation to Action in Addiction Recovery

Scenario:
John has been thinking about quitting smoking for several months. He feels motivated because he's noticed how smoking affects his breathing and overall health. However, John hasn't yet made any serious attempts to quit because he's worried about how difficult it will be.

Moving from Motivation to Action:

- **Exploring John's Motivation:** During a conversation with his healthcare provider, John shares that he wants to quit smoking because he's tired of feeling short of breath and is concerned about the long-term impact on his health. His provider responds, "It sounds like your health is really important to you, and quitting smoking is something you've been thinking about for a while."

- **Identifying Barriers:** John then talks about his fear of the withdrawal symptoms and the cravings he expects to experience. The provider might ask, "What do you think would help you manage those cravings when they come up?" John responds, "I'm not sure, but maybe I could try using nicotine gum or patches."

- **Planning the First Step:** With John's input, the provider helps him decide on a first step. John agrees to set a quit date for the following month and plans to use nicotine patches to help manage the withdrawal symptoms. He also commits to talking with a counselor for support during the quitting process.

In this example, John's motivation is already present, but he needs help turning that motivation into a clear plan of action. By helping him explore his concerns and identify practical solutions (such as nicotine patches and counseling), the provider helps John move from thinking about quitting to actually taking steps toward quitting.

Creating a Collaborative Change Plan

Creating a change plan is a collaborative process in MI. Rather than telling the person what they should do, the practitioner works together with the individual to co-create a plan that feels achievable, realistic, and aligned with their values. The change plan should be personalized, meaning it fits into the person's life and addresses their unique challenges and goals.

Key Elements of a Collaborative Change Plan

1. **Specific and Realistic Goals**
   - The change plan should include specific goals that are clearly defined. Instead of vague statements like "exercise more," the plan should include measurable goals such

as "walk for 30 minutes three times a week."

2. **Actionable Steps**
   - The plan should break down the goal into small, actionable steps. These steps should feel manageable to the person and not overwhelming.

3. **Addressing Barriers**
   - The change plan should take into account potential barriers and include strategies for overcoming them. For example, if time management is a concern, the plan might include strategies for fitting the goal into the person's daily routine.

4. **Flexible and Adjustable**
   - The plan should be flexible and allow for adjustments along the way. Change is often a process, and it's important to recognize that the person may need to revise their plan based on what they learn about themselves and their progress.

5. **Support and Accountability**
   - The change plan should include strategies for support and accountability. This could involve checking in with a counselor, coach, or friend, or using a journal to track progress.

Real-Life Example 3: Collaborative Change Plan in Career Development

Scenario:
Emily is a 35-year-old woman who feels stuck in her current job. She's been thinking about making a career change, but she's not sure where to start. She's motivated to find a new job that aligns with her passions, but she's also nervous about leaving the stability of her current position.

Creating a Collaborative Change Plan:

- **Clarifying the Goal:** Emily and her career coach begin by discussing what Emily wants from her career. Emily shares that she wants to find a job that allows her to be creative and work with a team. The coach asks, "What does your ideal job look like?" Emily responds, "I'd love to work in a creative field, like marketing or design."

- **Identifying the First Step:** Together, Emily and the coach explore possible first steps. Emily decides that her first step will be to research job opportunities in creative industries and update her resume to reflect her skills. The coach asks, "What's a manageable goal for the next week?" Emily commits to spending two hours over the weekend researching job listings and working on her resume.

- **Addressing Barriers:** Emily shares that she's worried about the financial impact of changing careers. The coach responds, "It sounds like finances are a big concern for you. What would help you feel more confident about managing that aspect?" Emily decides to meet with a financial planner to explore her options.

- **Support and Accountability:** To stay on track, Emily and her coach agree to meet once a week to review her progress. Emily will also keep a journal to document her thoughts and any challenges she encounters along the way.

Outcome:
Emily's change plan includes specific, actionable steps (researching jobs and updating her resume), addresses potential barriers (financial concerns), and includes a support system (weekly meetings with her coach). By creating this plan collaboratively, Emily feels empowered and confident about moving forward with her career change.

Real-Life Example 4: Collaborative Change Plan in Health Management

Scenario:
David is a 55-year-old man with Type 2 diabetes. His doctor has recommended that he make changes to his diet and exercise routine to manage his blood sugar levels. David feels motivated to improve his health but struggles to maintain healthy habits.

Creating a Collaborative Change Plan:

- **Clarifying the Goal:** During a conversation with his doctor, David expresses his desire to improve his health and avoid diabetes complications. The doctor asks, "What specific changes would you like to make to your lifestyle?" David responds, "I'd like to get more exercise and eat healthier meals, but I'm not sure how to start."

- **Identifying the First Step:** David and his doctor discuss possible ways to incorporate healthier habits into his daily routine. David decides to start by walking for 15 minutes after dinner three times a week and replacing sugary snacks with fruit. The doctor asks, "Does that feel like a realistic goal for you?" David agrees that it feels manageable.

- **Addressing Barriers:** David shares that he sometimes struggles to stay motivated, especially when he's tired after work. The doctor suggests, "What might help you stay motivated on those days?" David decides to set a reminder on his phone and invite his wife to join him on his evening walks for added support.

- **Support and Accountability:** David agrees to track his progress by writing down his exercise and meals in a journal. He also schedules a follow-up appointment with his doctor in one month to review his progress and make any necessary adjustments to the plan.

Outcome:
David's change plan is collaborative, realistic, and

personalized to his needs. It includes specific actions (walking after dinner and replacing sugary snacks), strategies for overcoming barriers (using reminders and inviting support from his wife), and a system for tracking progress (journaling and follow-up with his doctor).

The Role of Autonomy in Developing a Change Plan

One of the core principles of MI is supporting the person's autonomy—their ability to make their own choices and decisions. When developing a change plan, it's essential to ensure that the individual feels empowered and in control of the process. This means that the plan should be something the person feels ownership over, not something that is imposed on them by the practitioner.

Strategies for Supporting Autonomy

1. **Asking for Input:**
     - Rather than telling the person what they should do, ask for their input. For example, "What do you think would be a good first step for you?" or "What changes feel most realistic for you right now?"

2. **Collaborating on Solutions:**
     - Work together with the person to come up with strategies for overcoming challenges. For example, "It sounds like finding time to exercise has been difficult. What are some ways we could work around that?"

3. **Emphasizing Choice:**
    - Reinforce the idea that the person is in control of their decisions. For example, "It's completely up to you how you want to move forward. What feels right for you?"

Real-Life Example 5: Supporting Autonomy in a Change Plan

Scenario:
Maria is a 50-year-old woman who has been advised to reduce her alcohol consumption due to health concerns. Maria feels conflicted because while she wants to improve her health, she enjoys drinking socially with her friends.

Supporting Autonomy in the Change Plan:

- **Clarifying Maria's Priorities:** During a conversation with her healthcare provider, Maria shares her concerns about her drinking habits. The provider responds, "It sounds like your health is really important to you, but at the same time, you're not sure how to balance that with your social life."

- **Asking for Input:** Instead of prescribing a solution, the provider asks, "What do you think would be a good first step in reducing your drinking, while still enjoying time with your friends?" Maria suggests, "Maybe I could limit myself to one or two drinks when I'm out."

- **Collaborating on Solutions:** The provider then asks, "What strategies do you think might help you stick to that limit when you're out with friends?" Maria decides that she'll order water or a non-alcoholic drink in between alcoholic drinks to help her pace herself.
- **Emphasizing Choice:** Finally, the provider reminds Maria, "Remember, it's your decision how you want to approach this. You're in control of how you manage your drinking."

Outcome:
By supporting Maria's autonomy, the provider helps her feel more in control of her decisions. Maria's change plan is tailored to her specific needs and includes strategies that she feels confident in implementing.

Adjusting the Change Plan as Needed

It's important to recognize that change is not always a linear process. People may encounter setbacks or find that their original plan needs to be adjusted. MI encourages flexibility and adaptability in the change plan, allowing the individual to make changes as they learn more about themselves and their progress.

Real-Life Example 6: Adjusting the Change Plan

Scenario:
Jake is a 30-year-old man who has been trying to reduce his screen time by limiting his use of social media. His original change plan was to check social media only once a

day, but after a few weeks, Jake finds that this goal is too difficult to maintain.

Adjusting the Change Plan:

- **Checking in with Jake:** During a follow-up session, Jake shares that he's struggled to stick to his plan. The counselor responds, "It sounds like checking social media once a day was harder than you expected. What do you think might be a more realistic goal for you?"

- **Revising the Plan:** Jake decides to adjust his plan to allow for two short social media check-ins per day, which feels more manageable. The counselor affirms, "It sounds like this new plan feels like a better fit for your routine."

- **Encouraging Flexibility:** The counselor also reminds Jake, "It's completely normal to make adjustments along the way. The important thing is finding a plan that works for you."

Outcome:
By adjusting the change plan to fit Jake's needs, the counselor helps him stay motivated and continue making progress toward his goal. The flexibility of the plan allows Jake to find a balance that works for him.

Conclusion: Moving from Motivation to Action and Creating a Collaborative Change Plan

Developing a change plan is a collaborative, client-centered process that helps individuals move from motivation to actionable steps. In MI, the change plan is not imposed on the person but is co-created with their input, ensuring that it feels realistic, manageable, and aligned with their values. By breaking down the goal into specific, achievable steps, addressing potential barriers, and providing support and accountability, the change plan serves as a roadmap for success.

As seen in the real-life examples, a successful change plan involves:

- Clarifying the individual's goals and motivations
- Identifying manageable first steps
- Addressing barriers and challenges
- Supporting the person's autonomy and allowing for flexibility
- Providing ongoing support and accountability

By using these strategies, you can help individuals turn their motivation into action and create meaningful, lasting change in their lives.

Chapter 8: Real-Life Applications of MI

Motivational Interviewing (MI) is a counseling approach designed to help individuals resolve ambivalence and move toward change. Its core principle is working collaboratively with individuals, allowing them to explore their motivations and make decisions that align with their personal values and goals. MI has been used in a wide range of settings, including healthcare, addiction treatment, coaching, mentorship, education, and social work.

In this comprehensive explanation, we will explore real-life applications of MI, focusing on four key areas:

1. MI in health settings (smoking cessation, addiction)
2. MI in coaching and mentorship
3. MI in education and social work
4. Case studies and examples

Throughout this discussion, we will include real-life examples to show how MI is used in practice, making these concepts easy to understand and apply.

MI in Health Settings
MI for Smoking Cessation

Smoking is one of the most common health behaviors that people want to change, yet quitting can be incredibly challenging due to the addictive nature of nicotine and the emotional comfort that smoking often provides. MI has proven to be an effective approach in helping individuals quit smoking because it focuses on exploring ambivalence—those mixed feelings about wanting to quit but also enjoying smoking.

How MI Helps:

- MI helps individuals who smoke explore their desire to quit by focusing on their own reasons for change rather than imposing external pressure.

- Practitioners help individuals weigh the pros and cons of quitting versus continuing to smoke.

- MI techniques such as open-ended questions, affirmations, and reflective listening encourage individuals to talk about the benefits of quitting and the challenges they expect to face.

Real-Life Example: Smoking Cessation with MI

- **Scenario:** Lisa is a 35-year-old woman who has been smoking for over 15 years. She has tried to quit several times but hasn't been successful. Lisa feels torn because she knows smoking is bad for her health, but she enjoys it as a way to relax and cope with stress.

- **Using MI:** During a session with her healthcare provider, Lisa is encouraged to talk about her thoughts on quitting. The provider uses MI by asking, "What are some reasons you've thought about quitting?" Lisa responds, "Well, I know it's bad for my lungs, and I want to be around for my kids, but I don't think I can handle the cravings."

Instead of pushing Lisa to quit right away, the provider reflects her ambivalence: "It sounds like you really want to quit for your health and your family, but the cravings feel overwhelming." By acknowledging both sides of Lisa's struggle, the provider creates a safe space for her to continue exploring her motivations. Over time, Lisa feels more confident about making a quit plan because it's based on her own reasons for change.

MI for Addiction

Addiction is another area where MI is widely used. People struggling with addiction often experience ambivalence about quitting or reducing their substance use. MI's non-confrontational approach is particularly helpful in addiction treatment because it focuses on the person's own motivations for change, rather than telling them what they should do.

How MI Helps:

- MI allows individuals to talk about their reasons for change at their own pace, helping them resolve their ambivalence about quitting or reducing substance use.

- Practitioners help individuals explore the negative consequences of their addiction while also discussing the benefits of change.

- MI emphasizes empathy, avoiding judgment, and supporting the individual's autonomy, which is essential in addiction treatment.

Real-Life Example: Addiction Recovery with MI

- **Scenario:** John is a 45-year-old man who has been struggling with alcohol addiction for over a decade. He knows that his drinking has caused problems in his relationships and at work, but he feels uncertain about whether he's ready to quit.

- **Using MI:** During a session with his addiction counselor, John talks about his drinking habits. The counselor uses MI by asking, "What are some of the things you enjoy about drinking, and what are some things you don't like?" John says, "I like how it helps me relax, but I hate how I feel the next morning and how it's affecting my marriage."

The counselor reflects this ambivalence: "It sounds like drinking has been a way for you to unwind, but it's also starting to take a toll on your health and relationships." By focusing on John's mixed feelings, the counselor helps him explore his reasons for wanting to quit without feeling pressured. Over several sessions, John begins to develop a plan for cutting back on his drinking and eventually enters a treatment program when he feels ready.

MI in Coaching and Mentorship

Motivational Interviewing is also highly effective in coaching and mentorship, where the goal is often to help individuals achieve personal or professional growth. Whether the focus is on career development, life coaching, or sports coaching, MI provides a framework for helping individuals tap into their internal motivations and take ownership of their goals.

MI in Career Coaching

In career coaching, individuals often seek guidance in making important career decisions, setting goals, and overcoming obstacles. MI helps coaches guide clients in identifying their values and aspirations, exploring any ambivalence they may feel, and creating actionable plans for achieving their goals.

How MI Helps:

- MI helps individuals clarify their career goals by focusing on their internal motivations and values.
- Coaches use open-ended questions to explore the client's strengths, passions, and barriers to success.
- MI techniques such as reflective listening and affirmations help clients feel supported and encouraged as they navigate their career path.

Real-Life Example: Career Coaching with MI

- **Scenario:** Emily is a 30-year-old woman who feels stuck in her current job. She's been thinking about pursuing a career change but feels unsure about what direction to take. She's also worried about leaving the security of her current position.

- **Using MI:** Emily's career coach uses MI to help her explore her feelings about her job. The coach asks open-ended questions like, "What aspects of your current job do you enjoy, and what would you like to change?" Emily replies, "I like working with people, but I feel unfulfilled. I've been thinking about going into marketing, but I'm afraid of making the leap."

The coach reflects Emily's ambivalence: "It sounds like you enjoy connecting with people and are interested in marketing, but the uncertainty of a career change is holding you back." By using MI, the coach helps Emily explore her options without pressuring her to make a decision right away. Over time, Emily gains clarity about her next steps and begins taking small actions toward pursuing a career in marketing.

MI in Sports Coaching

In sports coaching, MI can be used to help athletes develop the mental and emotional skills needed to achieve their goals. Athletes often face pressure, self-doubt, and performance anxiety, and MI can help them explore their motivations, set realistic goals, and stay committed to their training.

How MI Helps:

- MI helps athletes reflect on their personal goals and reasons for participating in their sport, rather than focusing solely on external pressures.

- Coaches use MI to guide athletes in setting specific, achievable goals that align with their values.

- MI encourages athletes to explore their ambivalence about training, performance, or competition, helping them stay motivated over the long term.

Real-Life Example: Sports Coaching with MI

- **Scenario:** Jake is a 17-year-old soccer player who has been struggling with motivation. He loves the sport but has been feeling burned out from the constant pressure to perform. He's considering quitting, but he's not sure if that's what he really wants.

- **Using MI:** Jake's coach uses MI to help him explore his feelings about soccer. The coach asks, "What do you enjoy most about playing soccer, and what's been difficult for you lately?" Jake responds, "I love being part of a team, but the pressure to win all the time is getting to me. I'm not sure if it's worth it anymore."

The coach reflects Jake's ambivalence: "It sounds like you really value the teamwork and camaraderie, but the pressure has been making it hard to enjoy the game." By helping Jake explore both sides of his feelings, the coach creates a supportive space for Jake to think about what he wants from soccer. Over time, Jake decides to focus on enjoying the game and sets new, more manageable goals for his performance.

MI in Education and Social Work

Motivational Interviewing is also widely used in education and social work, where the goal is often to help individuals, especially young people or those facing challenges, make positive life changes. In these settings, MI can help students, clients, or families work through ambivalence about their education, behaviors, or life circumstances and take steps toward improvement.

MI in Education

In education, MI can be used by teachers, school counselors, and administrators to support students in making decisions about their academic progress, behavior, and personal development. MI can be especially helpful for students who are struggling with motivation, attendance, or academic performance.

How MI Helps:

- MI helps students explore their reasons for wanting to succeed in school, focusing on their own motivations rather than external expectations.

- Teachers and counselors use MI to support students in setting academic goals and overcoming barriers to success.

- MI fosters a collaborative and non-judgmental approach to addressing behavioral issues, helping students take ownership of their choices.

Real-Life Example: MI in Education

- **Scenario:** Sarah is a 16-year-old high school student who has been skipping classes and falling behind in her studies. She's unsure about her future and feels disconnected from school. Her school counselor uses MI to help her explore her feelings about her education.

- **Using MI:** The counselor asks Sarah, "What are your thoughts about school right now, and how do you see it fitting into your future?" Sarah responds, "I don't know. I feel like school isn't for me, but I know I need to graduate to get a decent job."

The counselor reflects Sarah's ambivalence: "It sounds like you're feeling disconnected from school, but at the same time, you see the importance of graduating for your future." Through this MI conversation, Sarah begins to explore her options, such as enrolling in a vocational program that aligns with her interests, which helps her re-engage with her education.

MI in Social Work

Social workers often work with individuals and families who are facing significant challenges, such as poverty, homelessness, addiction, or mental health issues. MI can help social workers guide their clients in exploring their strengths, setting goals, and making positive changes in their lives.

How MI Helps:

- MI helps clients reflect on their own reasons for making changes, rather than feeling pressured by external factors.

- Social workers use MI to empower clients by affirming their strengths and encouraging self-efficacy.

- MI encourages clients to set realistic goals and take small steps toward change, reducing the overwhelming feeling of addressing multiple challenges at once.

Real-Life Example: MI in Social Work

- **Scenario:** Maria is a 28-year-old single mother who has been struggling to find stable housing for her family. She's been feeling overwhelmed and discouraged, and she's unsure how to move forward.

- **Using MI:** Maria's social worker uses MI to help her explore her strengths and options. The social worker asks, "What are some things you've done in the past that have helped you manage difficult situations?" Maria responds, "I've always been able to find temporary housing, but it's hard to make it last."

The social worker reflects Maria's resourcefulness: "It sounds like you've been really resourceful in finding temporary housing, even though it's been tough to find something long-term." By affirming Maria's strengths, the social worker helps her feel more confident about exploring new housing options and setting a plan for finding stable housing.

Case Studies and Examples

To further illustrate how MI is applied in real-life situations, let's explore a few case studies that demonstrate the effectiveness of MI in different settings.

Case Study 1: MI in Smoking Cessation

Background:
David is a 50-year-old man who has smoked for 30 years. He knows that quitting would improve his health, but he has tried several times before without success. David feels conflicted because he enjoys smoking but also worries about the impact on his health.

Using MI:
David's healthcare provider uses MI to help him explore his ambivalence about quitting. The provider asks, "What are some of the reasons you've thought about quitting smoking, and what are some of the reasons you've continued?" David responds, "I know it's bad for my lungs, and my wife wants me to quit, but it's my way of relaxing after work."

The provider reflects David's ambivalence: "It sounds like you're concerned about your health and your relationship with your wife, but smoking has also been a way for you to relax." Over the course of several sessions, David begins to explore alternative ways to manage stress, such as exercising or meditating, and sets a quit date. With support from his healthcare provider, David successfully quits smoking and finds new ways to relax.

Case Study 2: MI in Addiction Treatment

Background:
Alex is a 32-year-old man who has been using opioids for several years. He has experienced multiple relapses and feels unsure about whether he can quit. Alex's addiction has strained his relationships with his family and affected his ability to hold down a job.

Using MI:
During a session with his addiction counselor, Alex expresses his doubts about quitting. The counselor uses MI by asking, "What are some of the reasons you've thought about quitting, and what's holding you back?" Alex replies, "I know I need to quit for my family, but I'm afraid I won't be able to handle the withdrawal symptoms."

The counselor reflects Alex's ambivalence: "It sounds like you want to quit for your family, but you're worried about how hard the process will be." By focusing on Alex's mixed feelings, the counselor helps him explore his motivations for change and consider treatment options, such as medication-assisted therapy, to help manage withdrawal. Over time, Alex enters a treatment program and begins his recovery journey.

Case Study 3: MI in Education

Background:
Jasmine is a 17-year-old student who has been skipping school and is at risk of not graduating. She feels disengaged from her studies and isn't sure if school is the right path for her.

Using MI:
Jasmine's school counselor uses MI to help her explore her thoughts about school. The counselor asks, "What's been going on for you with school lately, and how do you feel about your future?" Jasmine replies, "I don't see the point. I'm not sure if I even want to go to college."

The counselor reflects Jasmine's ambivalence: "It sounds like you're feeling unsure about your future and whether school is the right path for you." By using MI, the counselor helps Jasmine explore her options, such as vocational training, and set goals that align with her interests. Jasmine re-engages with her studies and starts working toward a plan for her future.

Conclusion: Real-Life Applications of MI

Motivational Interviewing is a versatile and effective approach that can be applied in a wide range of real-life settings, including healthcare, addiction treatment, coaching, mentorship, education, and social work. By focusing on the individual's internal motivations, MI helps people explore their ambivalence, set goals, and take action in a way that feels meaningful and empowering.

The key to MI's success lies in its non-judgmental, collaborative approach, which helps individuals feel heard, respected, and supported as they navigate the process of change. Whether the goal is quitting smoking, overcoming addiction, making a career change, or re-engaging with education, MI provides a powerful framework for helping individuals achieve lasting, positive change in their lives.

Chapter 9: Common Mistakes in MI

Motivational Interviewing (MI) is an effective approach to helping individuals work through their ambivalence and make positive changes in their lives. However, like any skill, MI requires practice and self-awareness. Beginners can sometimes make mistakes that hinder progress or fail to use the full potential of MI.

This comprehensive explanation will explore the most common mistakes that beginners in MI may encounter, provide real-life examples to illustrate these pitfalls, and offer strategies for avoiding these mistakes. The goal is to help you become more effective in using MI by highlighting common challenges and giving you practical tools to overcome them.

The Righting Reflex
Trying to "Fix" the Person's Problems

What is the Righting Reflex?

One of the most common mistakes beginners make in MI is the "righting reflex," which refers to the natural tendency to want to fix the other person's problems or tell them what to do. When someone expresses a challenge or struggle, our instinct might be to offer solutions or advice right away. While this is done with good intentions, it can backfire because the person may feel pressured, judged, or like their autonomy is being taken away.

Why It's a Problem:

The righting reflex can increase resistance. When people feel like they are being told what to do, they may become defensive or resistant, even if they know the advice is sound. MI is based on the principle of collaboration, where the person being helped is the expert in their own life. The role of the practitioner is to guide the conversation, not to direct it.

Real-Life Example: The Righting Reflex in Smoking Cessation

- **Scenario:** John is a 40-year-old man who has been smoking for 20 years. He tells his healthcare provider, "I know I should quit, but I just enjoy it too much."

- **Mistake (Righting Reflex):** The provider responds, "You really need to quit smoking. It's bad for your health, and there are so many ways to help you stop. You should try nicotine patches or gum."

- **Result:** John feels like he's being told what to do, which makes him more defensive. He responds, "I've tried all that before. It doesn't work."

How to Avoid the Righting Reflex:

- Instead of trying to fix the problem, use **reflective listening** to show that you understand the person's perspective.

- Focus on **open-ended questions** that allow the individual to explore their own motivations for change.

- Avoid giving unsolicited advice. If the person asks for advice, offer it in a collaborative way, such as, "Would it be helpful if we explored some strategies together?"

Real-Life Example (Corrected):

- **Scenario (Revisited):** John says, "I know I should quit, but I just enjoy it too much."

- **Using MI:** The provider responds with reflective listening: "It sounds like part of you wants to quit because you know it's better for your health, but another part of you really enjoys smoking."

- **Result:** John feels heard and validated. He responds, "Yeah, it's hard to let go of it, but I know I need to think about quitting."

Overloading the Conversation
What Happens When You Ask Too Many Questions?

Asking questions is an essential part of MI, but beginners often fall into the trap of asking too many questions in rapid succession. This can make the conversation feel more like an interrogation than a supportive dialogue. The person might feel overwhelmed or pressured to provide answers quickly, which can disrupt the flow of the conversation.

Why It's a Problem:

When the conversation is dominated by questions, it leaves little room for the person to reflect on their thoughts and feelings. It also shifts the focus away from the individual's internal motivations and makes the interaction feel like a checklist of questions that need to be answered. This can hinder the development of rapport and trust.

Real-Life Example: Overloading with Questions in Weight Loss Coaching

- **Scenario:** Sarah is a 35-year-old woman who is trying to lose weight. She tells her coach, "I've been struggling to stick to my diet."

- **Mistake (Too Many Questions):** The coach responds with a series of rapid-fire questions: "What have you been eating? How often do you exercise? Have you been tracking your calories? Why do you think you're struggling?"

- **Result:** Sarah feels overwhelmed and starts giving short, defensive answers: "I don't know. I've just been busy."

How to Avoid Overloading with Questions:

- Use a balance of **open-ended questions** and **reflective listening**. After asking a question, give the person time to think and respond.

- Focus on **quality** rather than **quantity** of questions. A few well-placed open-ended questions can lead to deeper, more meaningful conversations than a long series of questions.

- Allow for **silence**. Giving the person space to think before responding can lead to richer answers.

Real-Life Example (Corrected):

- **Scenario (Revisited):** Sarah says, "I've been struggling to stick to my diet."

- **Using MI:** The coach asks one open-ended question: "What do you think has made it difficult to stick to your diet lately?"

- **Result:** Sarah reflects and responds, "I think it's because I've been really stressed at work, and I've been turning to comfort food." This opens the door for a deeper conversation about how stress affects her eating habits.

Not Allowing Enough Time for the Person to Reflect

Why Reflection is Important:

One of the core principles of MI is allowing the person to reflect on their thoughts, feelings, and motivations. Beginners often rush through the conversation, jumping from one topic to another without giving the individual enough time to process their thoughts. MI works best when people are given the space to explore their ambivalence and come to their own conclusions.

Why It's a Problem:

When the conversation moves too quickly, the person may not have the opportunity to fully consider their options, motivations, or barriers to change. This can prevent them from reaching important insights about their behavior. Additionally, rushing the conversation can make the person feel like they are being pushed toward a decision, which can lead to resistance.

Real-Life Example: Rushing Through Reflection in Addiction Counseling

- **Scenario:** Alex is a 28-year-old man who is struggling with alcohol addiction. He tells his counselor, "I've been thinking about cutting back on drinking, but I'm not sure if I can do it."

- **Mistake (Rushing Through Reflection):** The counselor quickly jumps in and says, "Well, there are plenty of resources available to help you quit. Let's talk about some options."

- **Result:** Alex feels like his concerns weren't fully addressed, and he becomes hesitant to engage further. He says, "I don't know. I'm not sure if I'm ready."

How to Avoid Rushing Through Reflection:

- Use **reflective listening** to help the person explore their ambivalence. For example, "It sounds like part of you wants to cut back, but another part is unsure if it's possible."

- Allow for **pauses** and **silence** in the conversation. Silence gives the person time to reflect on their thoughts without feeling pressured to respond immediately.

- **Slow down the pace** of the conversation. Encourage the person to take their time in exploring their feelings and thoughts.

Real-Life Example (Corrected):

- **Scenario (Revisited):** Alex says, "I've been thinking about cutting back on drinking, but I'm not sure if I can do it."

- **Using MI:** The counselor responds with reflective listening: "It sounds like you're thinking about making a change, but you're also feeling uncertain about whether you can follow through."

- **Result:** Alex feels understood and takes a moment to reflect. He responds, "Yeah, I've tried before, but it's been hard. I want to try again, though."

---

4. Focusing on the Problem Instead of the Person

What Happens When You Focus on the Problem?

It's easy for beginners in MI to become overly focused on the problem that the person is facing rather than the individual's experience, values, and motivations. When the conversation centers only on the problem (such as smoking, overeating, or substance use), it can feel like the person's identity is being reduced to that one issue.

Why It's a Problem:

Focusing too much on the problem can make the individual feel like they are being judged or criticized. It can also limit the conversation to surface-level solutions without exploring the deeper motivations or emotions behind the behavior. MI is most effective when it takes a holistic approach, focusing on the person as a whole rather than just the problem.

Real-Life Example: Focusing on the Problem in Smoking Cessation

- **Scenario:** Megan is a 45-year-old woman who wants to quit smoking. She tells her healthcare provider, "I know I need to quit, but it's really hard for me."

- **Mistake (Focusing on the Problem):** The provider immediately focuses on the smoking behavior: "Well, smoking is really bad for your health. Have you considered nicotine patches or medication to help you quit?"

- **Result:** Megan feels like her provider is only interested in her smoking, not her as a person. She responds, "Yeah, I've tried those things before. They didn't work."

How to Avoid Focusing Solely on the Problem:

- Use **open-ended questions** that focus on the person's values, experiences, and feelings. For example, "What's important to you about quitting smoking, and what do you hope will change in your life if you quit?"

- **Affirm the person's strengths** and efforts. Recognize that they are more than just their problem behavior.
- Explore the **individual's broader life context**, including their goals, relationships, and interests, rather than only focusing on the behavior they want to change.

Real-Life Example (Corrected):

- **Scenario (Revisited):** Megan says, "I know I need to quit, but it's really hard for me."
- **Using MI:** The provider responds, "It sounds like quitting smoking is something you really want to do, but it's been a difficult process for you. What's most important to you about quitting?"
- **Result:** Megan feels heard and responds, "I want to quit so I can be healthier for my kids. I've tried before, but it's hard to stay motivated."

---

5. Offering Advice Too Soon

Why Offering Advice Too Soon is a Pitfall:

Beginners in MI may feel the urge to offer advice or solutions too early in the conversation. While it's natural to want to help, offering advice before the person has had the chance to explore their own thoughts and feelings can shut down the conversation and reduce the person's sense of autonomy.

Why It's a Problem:

Offering advice too soon can make the person feel like they are being directed or controlled, rather than being allowed to explore their own options. It can also undermine the person's confidence in their ability to come up with their own solutions. MI is based on the principle that people are more likely to make lasting changes when they are involved in the decision-making process.

Real-Life Example: Offering Advice Too Soon in Exercise Coaching

- **Scenario:** Mike is a 50-year-old man who has been thinking about starting an exercise routine. He tells his coach, "I know I should be more active, but I don't have the time."

- **Mistake (Offering Advice Too Soon):** The coach responds, "You should start by doing short workouts in the morning before work. You could also try joining a gym."

- **Result:** Mike feels like the coach isn't listening to his concerns about time. He responds, "I've tried that before, but it didn't fit into my schedule."

How to Avoid Offering Advice Too Soon:

- Before offering advice, use **open-ended questions** and **reflective listening** to fully explore the person's thoughts and feelings.

- If the person asks for advice, offer it in a collaborative way by asking for permission. For example, "Would you like to explore some strategies for fitting exercise into your schedule?"

- Use **affirmations** to recognize the person's strengths and efforts before offering suggestions.

Real-Life Example (Corrected):

- **Scenario (Revisited):** Mike says, "I know I should be more active, but I don't have the time."
- **Using MI:** The coach responds, "It sounds like you've been thinking about starting an exercise routine, but you're feeling really pressed for time."
- **Result:** Mike feels heard and responds, "Yeah, between work and family, it's hard to fit it in." This opens the door for a deeper conversation about how Mike can manage his time and prioritize his health.

---

6. Ignoring or Minimizing Ambivalence

What is Ambivalence?

Ambivalence is the feeling of being stuck between two opposing desires or motivations. For example, a person may want to quit smoking because they know it's bad for their health but also enjoy smoking as a way to relax. Beginners in MI sometimes make the mistake of ignoring or minimizing ambivalence, focusing only on the desire for change without acknowledging the competing feelings.

Why It's a Problem:

Ignoring ambivalence can lead to resistance because the person may feel like their concerns or conflicting feelings are not being taken seriously. MI is most effective when the person's ambivalence is openly explored, allowing them to work through their mixed feelings and come to their own conclusions.

Real-Life Example: Ignoring Ambivalence in Addiction Recovery

- **Scenario:** Alex is a 30-year-old man who is thinking about quitting drinking. He tells his counselor, "I know I need to quit, but I just enjoy drinking too much."

- **Mistake (Ignoring Ambivalence):** The counselor responds, "It's great that you're thinking about quitting! Let's talk about how you can get started."

- **Result:** Alex feels like the counselor isn't acknowledging his enjoyment of drinking, so he becomes resistant and says, "I'm not sure if I'm ready to quit."

How to Avoid Ignoring Ambivalence:

- Use **double-sided reflections** to acknowledge both sides of the person's ambivalence. For example, "It sounds like part of you really wants to quit, but another part of you enjoys drinking and isn't sure if you're ready."

- Encourage the person to talk openly about their mixed feelings. For example, "What do you think are the benefits of drinking, and what are the downsides?"

- **Validate** the person's ambivalence and reassure them that it's normal to feel conflicted about making a change.

Real-Life Example (Corrected):

- **Scenario (Revisited):** Alex says, "I know I need to quit, but I just enjoy drinking too much."

- **Using MI:** The counselor responds with a double-sided reflection: "It sounds like you're feeling torn between wanting to quit for your health and still enjoying drinking as a way to relax."

- **Result:** Alex feels understood and responds, "Yeah, it's hard to give it up. I know I should quit, but it's tough to let go."

Conclusion: Avoiding Common Mistakes in MI

Motivational Interviewing is a powerful approach for helping individuals make positive changes in their lives, but it requires skill and practice. By avoiding common mistakes such as the righting reflex, overloading the conversation with questions, rushing through reflection, focusing too much on the problem, offering advice too soon, and ignoring ambivalence, you can become a more effective MI practitioner.

The key to success in MI is to remain patient, empathetic, and collaborative. By listening carefully, using reflective listening, and allowing the person to explore their own motivations, you can create a supportive environment that fosters meaningful change. As you continue to practice MI, these common pitfalls will become easier to recognize and avoid, allowing you to build stronger connections and guide individuals toward lasting change.

Chapter 10: Practicing MI in Everyday Life

Motivational Interviewing (MI) is often thought of as a technique used by professionals in fields such as healthcare, counseling, and social work. However, the principles of MI can be incredibly useful in everyday conversations as well. Whether you're talking with friends, family members, colleagues, or even acquaintances, MI can help create more meaningful, supportive, and productive conversations. By integrating MI into your daily interactions, you can build stronger connections, help others explore their thoughts and feelings, and support them in making positive changes.

In this comprehensive explanation, we will explore how to practice MI in everyday life, how to integrate MI techniques into daily conversations, and how to build confidence through consistent practice. We will provide real-life examples to make these concepts easy to understand and apply.

Understanding the Basics of Motivational Interviewing (MI)

Before diving into how to integrate MI into everyday conversations, it's essential to review the basic principles of MI. At its core, MI is a person-centered communication style designed to help individuals explore their own motivations for change. The approach emphasizes empathy, collaboration, and respect for the individual's autonomy.

Key elements of MI include:

1. **Open-ended questions**: Asking questions that encourage deeper reflection rather than simple yes/no answers.
2. **Reflective listening**: Listening carefully and reflecting back what the other person is saying to show understanding.
3. **Affirmations**: Recognizing and affirming the person's strengths, efforts, and positive attributes.
4. **Summarizing**: Pulling together key points from the conversation to reinforce what the person has shared.
5. **Avoiding the righting reflex**: Resisting the urge to "fix" the person or offer unsolicited advice.

MI is most effective when used in a collaborative, non-judgmental manner, helping individuals tap into their own motivations and resources.

Integrating MI into Daily Conversations

Integrating MI techniques into your everyday conversations can improve your interactions with others and help you build stronger relationships. While you may not need to use MI in every conversation, knowing how to incorporate MI principles can make a significant difference in discussions where someone is exploring their feelings, facing challenges, or considering a change.

1. Using Open-Ended Questions

Open-ended questions are one of the most fundamental techniques in MI, and they can easily be integrated into daily conversations. Open-ended questions encourage the other person to reflect and expand on their thoughts, leading to a deeper and more meaningful exchange. These questions are especially useful when someone is dealing with uncertainty, ambivalence, or emotional challenges.

Real-Life Example 1: Supporting a Friend's Decision

- **Scenario:** Your friend Sarah is thinking about leaving her job but feels unsure about whether it's the right decision. Instead of offering advice right away, you can use open-ended questions to help her explore her feelings.

- **You might say:** "What's been on your mind about leaving your job?" or "What do you think would change for you if you decided to make a move?"

- **Result:** Sarah responds by reflecting on her feelings, saying, "I think I'd feel more fulfilled if I moved to a new position, but I'm worried about taking the risk." By asking open-ended questions, you've helped Sarah explore her thoughts more deeply.

Real-Life Example 2: Talking with a Family Member

- **Scenario:** Your sibling is thinking about adopting a new hobby but is hesitant because they feel they might not be good at it.

- **You might say:** "What excites you about trying out this new hobby?" or "What would it look like if you gave it a try?"
- **Result:** Your sibling starts to reflect on their interest in the hobby and says, "I think it would be fun, but I'm nervous about being a beginner." By asking open-ended questions, you've allowed your sibling to explore both the excitement and the concerns they feel.

2. Reflective Listening

Reflective listening is another powerful MI technique that can enhance your everyday conversations. Reflective listening involves carefully listening to what the other person is saying and then reflecting it back to them in your own words. This shows that you are fully engaged in the conversation and helps the person feel heard and understood.

Real-Life Example 1: Listening to a Colleague

- **Scenario:** A colleague is feeling stressed about an upcoming project deadline and shares their concerns with you. Instead of jumping in with solutions, you use reflective listening.
- **You might say:** "It sounds like you're feeling overwhelmed by everything that needs to get done before the deadline."
- **Result:** Your colleague responds, "Yes, exactly. I'm just worried that I won't be able to finish everything on time." Reflective listening has helped

your colleague feel heard, and they are now more open to discussing their concerns further.

Real-Life Example 2: Talking with a Partner

- **Scenario:** Your partner is frustrated about a disagreement they had with a family member. Instead of offering advice or taking sides, you reflect their feelings.

- **You might say:** "It seems like you're feeling hurt by the conversation and unsure about how to move forward."

- **Result:** Your partner says, "Yes, I don't know how to resolve it, and I don't want things to stay like this." Reflective listening helps your partner feel supported, allowing them to express their emotions more freely.

3. Offering Affirmations

Affirmations are positive, supportive statements that recognize the other person's strengths, efforts, or values. In everyday conversations, affirmations can be used to build the other person's confidence, acknowledge their efforts, and show appreciation for their abilities.

Real-Life Example 1: Encouraging a Friend

- **Scenario:** Your friend has been working hard on a personal project but is feeling discouraged because they haven't seen the results they were hoping for.

- **You might say:** "You've put so much effort into this project, and it's clear how dedicated you are. It's amazing to see your perseverance."
- **Result:** Your friend feels recognized and appreciated for their hard work, which boosts their confidence and motivation to continue working on the project.

Real-Life Example 2: Supporting a Family Member

- **Scenario:** Your parent has been trying to adopt healthier habits, such as exercising regularly and eating better. They mention feeling like they're not making enough progress.
- **You might say:** "You've been so committed to making these changes, and even though it's been tough, you're sticking with it. That takes a lot of determination."
- **Result:** Your parent feels validated and is reminded of the effort they've been putting in, which encourages them to keep going.

4. Avoiding the Righting Reflex

The righting reflex refers to the instinct to "fix" someone's problems or offer solutions right away. In everyday conversations, it's easy to fall into the trap of trying to solve the other person's issues, especially if they are sharing a problem or a challenge. However, MI encourages us to avoid the righting reflex and instead focus on listening, reflecting, and asking open-ended questions.

Real-Life Example 1: Supporting a Friend in a Relationship

- **Scenario:** Your friend is having relationship difficulties and expresses uncertainty about whether they should stay in the relationship.

- **Mistake (Righting Reflex):** If you immediately offer advice and say, "You should leave if you're not happy," your friend might feel like their concerns haven't been fully explored.

- **Using MI Instead:** You could say, "It sounds like you're feeling really conflicted about whether to stay or leave. What's been most challenging for you?" This allows your friend to explore their feelings in more depth without feeling pressured to make a decision.

Real-Life Example 2: Talking with a Colleague About Work

- **Scenario:** A colleague is frustrated with their workload and feels like they're not being recognized for their contributions. Instead of jumping in with suggestions for how they can improve their work-life balance, you use MI principles.

- **You might say:** "It sounds like you've been working really hard, but you're not getting the recognition you deserve. How do you feel about that?" This approach encourages your colleague to reflect on their feelings and explore their options, rather than feeling like they're being told what to do.

Building Confidence Through Practice

Like any skill, becoming confident in using MI requires consistent practice. The more you integrate MI techniques into your everyday conversations, the more natural they will become. Over time, you'll find that you are better able to listen, respond empathetically, and support others in exploring their own motivations and solutions.

1. Start Small and Build Gradually

When first practicing MI in everyday life, it's important to start small and build your skills gradually. You don't need to use MI techniques in every conversation, but you can begin by incorporating one or two MI principles in situations where they are most needed.

Real-Life Example: Starting Small with MI

- **Scenario:** Your friend is thinking about starting a new exercise routine but feels hesitant. Instead of jumping in with advice, you decide to start by using reflective listening and open-ended questions.

- **You might say:** "It sounds like you're interested in getting more active, but you're not sure where to start. What kind of exercise are you thinking about trying?"

- **Result:** Your friend begins to explore their options and feels more comfortable discussing their thoughts. By starting small and focusing on one MI technique (open-ended questions), you've helped your friend feel more at ease.

As you become more comfortable with MI, you can start incorporating additional techniques, such as affirmations and summarizing, into your conversations.

2. Reflect on Your Conversations

After using MI techniques in a conversation, take a moment to reflect on how it went. Ask yourself questions such as:

- Did I ask open-ended questions that encouraged the other person to explore their thoughts?
- Did I use reflective listening to show that I was fully engaged?
- Did I avoid the righting reflex and allow the person to find their own solutions?
- Did I offer affirmations that recognized the other person's strengths and efforts?

By reflecting on your conversations, you can identify areas where you're doing well and areas where you can improve.

Real-Life Example: Reflecting on a Conversation

- **Scenario:** You had a conversation with a friend who was struggling with a personal issue. You used reflective listening and avoided offering advice.
- **Reflection:** After the conversation, you reflect on how it went. You realize that your friend seemed more open and willing to talk because you didn't jump in with advice right away. You also notice that

your reflective listening helped your friend feel understood.

By reflecting on the conversation, you've gained insight into how MI can positively impact your interactions.

3. Practice with a Partner or Friend

One of the best ways to build confidence in using MI is to practice with a partner or friend. You can engage in role-playing exercises where one person shares a challenge or goal, and the other practices using MI techniques, such as open-ended questions, reflective listening, and affirmations.

Real-Life Example: Practicing MI with a Partner

- **Scenario:** You and a friend decide to practice MI together. One person shares a personal challenge (such as balancing work and life), and the other uses MI techniques to support them in exploring their feelings and motivations.

- **You might say:** "It sounds like you've been feeling really stretched thin between work and personal responsibilities. How do you think you could create more balance?"

- **Result:** Through this practice exercise, you and your friend gain experience in using MI techniques, which helps build your confidence in real-life conversations.

4. Embrace Feedback

As you practice MI, it's helpful to ask for feedback from the people you're interacting with. You can ask them how they felt during the conversation and whether they felt heard and supported. This feedback can provide valuable insights into how well you're using MI and where you might need to adjust your approach.

Real-Life Example: Seeking Feedback

- **Scenario:** After having a conversation with a family member about a decision they're considering, you ask for feedback on how they felt during the discussion.

- **You might say:** "I tried to listen and ask questions without giving advice. Did you feel like that approach helped you explore your thoughts?"

- **Result:** Your family member says, "Yeah, I felt like you really listened, and it helped me think through my options." This positive feedback reinforces that you're using MI effectively and encourages you to continue practicing.

5. Be Patient with Yourself

Like any new skill, learning to use MI effectively takes time and practice. It's important to be patient with yourself as you develop your MI abilities. There will be moments when you may slip into old habits, such as offering advice too soon or asking too many closed-ended questions. The key is to learn from these experiences and keep practicing.

Real-Life Example: Being Patient with Yourself

- **Scenario:** During a conversation with a friend, you realize that you accidentally offered advice before giving them the chance to fully explore their thoughts.
- **Reflection:** Instead of being hard on yourself, you reflect on the conversation and think about how you can approach it differently next time. You remind yourself that MI is a skill that takes time to master, and each conversation is an opportunity to improve.

The Impact of Practicing MI in Everyday Life

As you continue to practice MI in your daily interactions, you'll likely notice several positive changes in your relationships and communication. By integrating MI into your conversations, you can create an environment where people feel heard, understood, and supported. This can lead to deeper connections and more meaningful discussions.

Here are some potential benefits of practicing MI in everyday life:

1. Improved Listening Skills

MI emphasizes reflective listening, which helps you become a more attentive and empathetic listener. This can improve your relationships with others by showing that you value their thoughts and feelings.

2. Stronger Relationships

When people feel heard and understood, they are more likely to trust and open up to you. By using MI in your conversations, you can strengthen your relationships with friends, family, and colleagues.

3. Enhanced Problem-Solving

MI encourages individuals to explore their own solutions rather than relying on external advice. By helping others reflect on their motivations and options, you empower them to make decisions that are aligned with their values and goals.

4. Reduced Conflict

By avoiding the righting reflex and focusing on understanding rather than offering advice, you can reduce the likelihood of conflict in conversations. MI creates a collaborative atmosphere where people feel supported rather than judged.

5. Greater Personal Growth

Practicing MI not only helps others but also contributes to your personal growth. By developing your listening, communication, and empathy skills, you become a more effective communicator and a more compassionate person.

Conclusion: Practicing MI in Everyday Life

Motivational Interviewing is a versatile and powerful communication style that can be integrated into everyday conversations to create more meaningful, supportive, and empathetic interactions. By using techniques such as open-ended questions, reflective listening, affirmations, and avoiding the righting reflex, you can help others explore their thoughts, feelings, and motivations in a non-judgmental and collaborative way.

As you continue to practice MI in your daily life, you'll build confidence in your ability to support others without directing them or offering unsolicited advice. Whether you're talking with friends, family members, colleagues, or even strangers, MI can help you create a positive and respectful environment where people feel empowered to make decisions that align with their own values and goals.

Remember, MI is a skill that takes time and practice to develop, so be patient with yourself as you learn. Start small, reflect on your conversations, and seek feedback to continue improving. By integrating MI into your everyday life, you'll become a more effective communicator and build stronger, more supportive relationships with the people around you.

Conclusion

Integrating Motivational Interviewing (MI) into Everyday Life

Motivational Interviewing (MI) is not just a tool for professionals in counseling, healthcare, or social work—it is a communication style that can transform everyday conversations, helping to create more supportive, empathetic, and collaborative relationships. By integrating MI techniques into our daily lives, we can enhance the quality of our interactions with others, whether we're helping a friend through a difficult decision, supporting a family member in making a positive change, or fostering open dialogue with colleagues.

In this comprehensive guide, we've explored how MI principles can be applied in real-life situations, the common mistakes to avoid, and how to build confidence through consistent practice. Let's take a moment to review the key takeaways from our discussion:

1. Using MI to Foster Meaningful Conversations

One of the primary benefits of MI is that it encourages open, reflective conversations that allow people to explore their own thoughts, feelings, and motivations. Techniques such as open-ended questions and reflective listening help create an environment where the other person feels heard and understood, which is crucial for building trust and rapport. In daily interactions, these techniques can lead to richer, more meaningful conversations that go beyond surface-level exchanges.

For example, asking open-ended questions like, "What are your thoughts about this decision?" rather than "Do you think you'll do it?" encourages the person to reflect more deeply on their motivations. Reflective listening, where you mirror the person's feelings back to them, reinforces their sense that they are truly being listened to. These subtle shifts in communication style make a significant impact, turning everyday conversations into opportunities for self-reflection and growth.

2. Avoiding the Righting Reflex and Embracing Autonomy

A common pitfall in conversations is the "righting reflex," or the instinct to offer solutions, fix problems, or give advice too quickly. MI emphasizes the importance of avoiding this reflex, instead allowing the person to explore their own solutions. In everyday conversations, this means being patient, resisting the urge to "fix" someone's problems, and encouraging them to identify their own strengths and capabilities.

By avoiding the righting reflex, we give people the space to take ownership of their decisions. This not only builds their confidence but also leads to more sustainable outcomes because they are engaging with their own motivations, rather than simply following external advice. For example, instead of saying, "You should try doing this," an MI-informed approach would be, "What do you think might help in this situation?" This subtle shift puts the other person in control and respects their autonomy.

3. Building Confidence Through Affirmations and Support

Affirmations play a critical role in MI by acknowledging the other person's strengths, efforts, and positive qualities. When integrated into everyday conversations, affirmations can boost someone's confidence, reinforce their sense of competence, and encourage them to persevere in the face of challenges. Simple statements like, "You've worked really hard on this," or "It's clear how much you care about making this change," can have a profound effect on someone's motivation and self-esteem.

In everyday life, affirmations are a powerful way to build trust and support others. By affirming someone's strengths and efforts, we not only show that we recognize their abilities but also help them see themselves as capable of overcoming obstacles. This, in turn, encourages continued progress and engagement in their own journey of change.

4. Creating a Safe and Non-Judgmental Space

MI emphasizes empathy and non-judgment, which are essential for creating a supportive environment where people feel comfortable sharing their thoughts and emotions. In everyday conversations, practicing empathy means truly listening without judgment or criticism, and responding in ways that reflect understanding. By doing this, we create a space where people feel safe to express their concerns, explore their ambivalence, and consider the possibility of change.

This is especially important in conversations where someone may be feeling vulnerable, uncertain, or conflicted. For instance, if a friend is unsure about a life decision, rather than offering quick advice or passing judgment, you can say, "It sounds like you're feeling really torn about this decision, and that's completely understandable." This empathetic response helps the person feel validated and supported, making it easier for them to open up and work through their feelings.

5. Gaining Confidence Through Practice

Like any skill, becoming proficient in MI requires practice. The more you integrate MI principles into your everyday conversations, the more natural and confident you will become. As you gain experience, you'll develop a deeper understanding of how to listen reflectively, ask thoughtful open-ended questions, and provide affirmations that encourage others. Building confidence through practice allows you to apply MI techniques in a variety of settings—whether with family, friends, or colleagues—and make a meaningful difference in your interactions.

Practicing MI also involves reflecting on your conversations, seeking feedback from others, and continuously learning from each experience. By doing so, you become more aware of the nuances of communication, better equipped to handle sensitive or complex discussions, and more effective in supporting others as they navigate challenges and consider change.

6. Strengthening Relationships and Promoting Positive Change

Ultimately, practicing MI in everyday life strengthens relationships by fostering open, honest, and supportive communication. When people feel heard, understood, and respected, they are more likely to trust you, open up about their struggles, and seek your guidance. Moreover, MI promotes positive change by helping people identify their own motivations and solutions, rather than imposing external expectations or advice.

In both personal and professional relationships, the principles of MI create a foundation for collaboration and mutual respect. Whether you're helping a friend through a tough decision, supporting a family member in making lifestyle changes, or working with a colleague on a challenging project, MI equips you with the tools to engage in meaningful conversations that lead to deeper connections and lasting change.

Final Thoughts: Empowering Others Through Everyday MI

Motivational Interviewing is more than just a set of techniques—it's a mindset that prioritizes empathy, respect, and collaboration. By incorporating MI into everyday conversations, we empower others to explore their own motivations, make informed decisions, and take ownership of their actions. Whether you're talking with a loved one, a colleague, or a friend, the MI approach allows you to offer genuine support without taking control of the conversation.

The beauty of MI lies in its flexibility and adaptability. It can be used in a wide range of situations, from casual discussions to more serious conversations about life changes, goals, or challenges. No matter the context, the underlying principles of MI—open-ended questions, reflective listening, affirmations, and respecting autonomy—create an environment where people feel heard, valued, and capable of growth.

As you continue to practice MI, you'll find that it not only helps others but also enhances your own communication skills and deepens your relationships. Over time, MI becomes less about following a specific set of rules and more about embodying a way of interacting that is collaborative, empathetic, and empowering. By making MI a part of your everyday life, you create opportunities for personal growth, stronger connections, and positive change—for both yourself and those around you.

Reference

Apodaca, T.R. and Longabaugh, R., 2009. Mechanisms of change in motivational interviewing: A review and preliminary evaluation of the evidence. Addiction, 104(5), pp.705-715.

Arkowitz, H., Miller, W.R. and Rollnick, S., 2015. Motivational interviewing in the treatment of psychological problems. Annual Review of Clinical Psychology, 11, pp.123-141.

Berman, M.I., 2013. The effectiveness of motivational interviewing to reduce alcohol-related problems: a review of the evidence. Journal of Clinical Psychology, 69(5), pp.503-516.

Burke, B.L., Arkowitz, H. and Menchola, M., 2003. The efficacy of motivational interviewing: a meta-analysis of controlled clinical trials. Journal of Consulting and Clinical Psychology, 71(5), pp.843-861.

Catley, D., Harris, K.J., Mayo, M.S., Hall, S., Okuyemi, K.S. and Boardman, T., 2006. Motivational interviewing for encouraging cessation: A randomized controlled trial. Addiction, 101(7), pp.995-1005.

Dunn, C., Deroo, L. and Rivara, F.P., 2001. The use of brief interventions adapted from motivational interviewing across behavioral domains: a systematic review. Addiction, 96(12), pp.1725-1742.

Feldstein Ewing, S.W., Filbey, F.M., Sabbineni, A., Chandler, L.D. and Hutchison, K.E., 2011. How psychosocial interventions work: A preliminary look at what fMRI can tell us about the mechanism of action of motivational interviewing. Addiction, 106(2), pp.135-144.

Gaume, J., Bertholet, N., Faouzi, M., Gmel, G. and Daeppen, J.B., 2010. Counselor motivational interviewing skills and young adult change talk articulation during brief motivational intervention. Journal of Substance Abuse Treatment, 39(3), pp.272-281.

Heckman, C.J., Egleston, B.L. and Hofmann, M.T., 2010. Efficacy of motivational interviewing for smoking cessation: a systematic review and meta-analysis. Tobacco Control, 19(5), pp.410-416.

Hettema, J., Steele, J. and Miller, W.R., 2005. Motivational interviewing. Annual Review of Clinical Psychology, 1, pp.91-111.

Kealey, K.A., Ludman, E.J., Marek, P.M., Mann, S.L. and Bricker, J.B., 2007. Design and evaluation of an innovative motivationally based intervention to reduce smoking in high-risk adolescents. Journal of Pediatric Psychology, 32(3), pp.251-261.

Knight, K.M., McGowan, L., Dickens, C. and Bundy, C., 2006. A systematic review of motivational interviewing in physical health care settings. British Journal of Health Psychology, 11(2), pp.319-332.

Lai, D.T., Cahill, K., Qin, Y. and Tang, J.L., 2010. Motivational interviewing for smoking cessation. Cochrane Database of Systematic Reviews, (1).

Lundahl, B.W., Kunz, C., Brownell, C., Tollefson, D. and Burke, B.L., 2010. A meta-analysis of motivational interviewing: Twenty-five years of empirical studies. Research on Social Work Practice, 20(2), pp.137-160.

Lundahl, B. and Burke, B.L., 2009. The effectiveness and applicability of motivational interviewing: a practice-friendly review of four meta-analyses. Journal of Clinical Psychology, 65(11), pp.1232-1245.

Madson, M.B., Loignon, A.C. and Lane, C., 2009. Training in motivational interviewing: a systematic review. Journal of Substance Abuse Treatment, 36(1), pp.101-109.

Martins, R.K. and McNeil, D.W., 2009. Review of motivational interviewing in promoting health behaviors. Clinical Psychology Review, 29(4), pp.283-293.

Miller, W.R. and Rollnick, S., 2013. The effectiveness and theoretical underpinnings of motivational interviewing. Behavioral and Cognitive Psychotherapy, 41(1), pp.129-142.

Moyers, T.B., Martin, T., Manuel, J.K., Hendrickson, S.M. and Miller, W.R., 2005. Assessing competence in the use of motivational interviewing. Journal of Substance Abuse Treatment, 28(1), pp.19-26.

Naar, S., Safren, S.A. and Walters, S.T., 2018. Motivational interviewing and cognitive-behavioral therapy: Complementary approaches to behavior change. American Journal of Lifestyle Medicine, 12(1), pp.38-46.

Resnicow, K., DiIorio, C., Soet, J.E., Borrelli, B., Ernst, D., Hecht, J. and Ernst, D., 2002. Motivational interviewing in health promotion: It sounds like something is changing. Health Psychology, 21(5), pp.444-451.

Rollnick, S., Miller, W.R. and Butler, C.C., 2008. Motivational interviewing in health care: helping patients change behavior. American Journal of Health Promotion, 23(3), pp.10-20.

Rubak, S., Sandbaek, A., Lauritzen, T. and Christensen, B., 2005. Motivational interviewing: a systematic review and meta-analysis. British Journal of General Practice, 55(513), pp.305-312.

Soderlund, L.L., Madson, M.B., Rubak, S. and Nilsen, P., 2011. A systematic review of motivational interviewing training for general healthcare practitioners. Patient Education and Counseling, 84(1), pp.16-26.

Stott, N.C.H., Rees, M., Rollnick, S. and Pill, R.M., 1995. Innovation in clinical method: diabetes care and negotiating skills. Family Practice, 12(4), pp.413-418.

VanBuskirk, K.A. and Wetherell, J.L., 2014. Motivational interviewing with primary care populations: a systematic review and meta-analysis. Journal of Behavioral Medicine, 37(4), pp.768-780.

Walters, S.T., Ogle, R.L. and Martin, J.E., 2002. Perils and possibilities of group-based motivational interviewing. Cognitive and Behavioral Practice, 9(4), pp.277-285.

Walthouwer, M.J., Oenema, A., Lechner, L. and de Vries, H., 2015. Comparing a video and text version of a web-based computer-tailored intervention for obesity prevention: A randomized controlled trial. Journal of Medical Internet Research, 17(10), p.e236.

www.ingramcontent.com/pod-product-compliance
Lightning Source LLC
Chambersburg PA
CBHW070453090426
42735CB00012B/2536